LITTLE BOOK OF
USEFUL
SPELLS

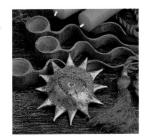

LITTLE BOOK OF

USEFUL
SPELLS

the good magic-maker's guide to
spellweaving

MARIANO KÄLFORS

southwater

This edition is published by Southwater

Southwater is an imprint of Anness Publishing Ltd
Hermes House, 88–89 Blackfriars Road, London SE1 8HA
tel. 020 7401 2077; fax 020 7633 9499
www.southwaterbooks.com; info@anness.com

UK agent: The Manning Partnership Ltd,
6 The Old Dairy, Melcombe Road, Bath BA2 3LR;
tel. 01225 478444; fax 01225 478440;
sales@manning-partnership.co.uk

UK distributor: Grantham Book Services Ltd,
Isaac Newton Way, Alma Park Industrial Estate, Grantham, Lincs NG31 9SD;
tel. 01476 541080; fax 01476 541061; orders@gbs.tbs-ltd.co.uk

North American agent/distributor:
National Book Network, 4501 Forbes Boulevard, Suite 200, Lanham, MD 20706;
tel. 301 459 3366; fax 301 429 5746; www.nbnbooks.com

Australian agent/distributor: Pan Macmillan Australia,
Level 18, St Martins Tower, 31 Market St, Sydney, NSW 2000;
tel. 1300 135 113; fax 1300 135 103; customer.service@macmillan.com.au

New Zealand agent/distributor: David Bateman Ltd,
30 Tarndale Grove, Off Bush Road, Albany, Auckland;
tel. (09) 415 7664; fax (09) 415 8892

A CIP catalogue record for this book is available from the British Library.

Publisher: Joanna Lorenz
Managing Editor: Judith Simons
Art Manager: Clare Reynolds
Consultant Editor: Raje Airey
Project Editor: Mariano Kälfors
Design: Pictures and Words
Editorial Reader: Richard McGinlay
Production Controller: Joanna King

Previously published as *White Witching*

Several spells have been adapted from Sally Morningstar's
Spellweaving, with additional text by Raje Airey.

10 9 8 7 6 5 4 3 2 1

Contents

Introduction   6

The basics   8

It's weird!   10
The wheel of the year   12
The sun and the moon   14
Elemental energies   16
Signs of the zodiac   18
The witch's tool kit   20
Countdown to magic   22
Sacred space   24
Meditation   26
Scrying   28
Inner journeys   29

The spells   30

Spells for ... angels and guides
Seeking guidance   32
Meeting your guardian angel   33
Angel blessings   34

Spells for ... protection and healing
Angel altar   35
Magic square of the sun   36
Psychic protection   37
Nature's healing powers   38
Stop the gossip   39
Mending a broken heart   40

Spells for ... self-empowerment
Removing obstacles   41
Strengthening willpower   42
Aura of confidence   43
Banishing the demons   44
Clear vision   45

Spells for ... luck and prosperity
Increasing abundance   46
Tree magic   47
Travel safely, travel well   48
Running smoothly   49

Spells for ... personal property
Bless this house   50
Clearing negative vibes   51
Finding what is lost   52
Make it go   53

Spells for ... love and romance
Dream lover   54
Magnetic attraction   55
Joining in love   56

Spells for ... friends and relationships
New friends   57
Removing conflict   58
Cutting the ties   59

Spells for ... moon magic
Drawing down the moon   60
Lunar wishes   61
Let it shine   62
Opening the inner gates   63

Index   64

Introduction

Today, ordinary people from all walks of life are practising witches. From the woman next door to the high-flying business executive, there are as many practising witches as there ever have been. These modern-day witches should not be confused with the ones who gave witchcraft a bad name. If you meet a witch it is much more likely to be a "white" one who uses the powers of magic for good, weaving spells to bring greater prosperity, health, happiness and wellbeing.

witches and spells

So what is a witch exactly? Some people think the word "witch" comes from an Old English word meaning "to know" but others say that it means "to cast a spell". A modern witch can be male or female, and you could say that it is someone who uses their "knowing" to bring about a desired result through the weaving of spells.

...being a witch today is not as outlandish as it may seem...

A spell is like a special recipe, uniquely designed to initiate a chain of events so as to make your wish come true. When a spell is cast, it is the intention and concentration of the spell-weaver that gives the spell its power. White witches only ever make spells that have a positive intention, and never ever seek to harm or cause pain to another. They believe in the "law of three": that what you put out will return threefold – so it makes good sense to only work with positive, loving energies as these are what will come back.

becoming a white witch

With patience and practice, anyone can be a white witch. It's about developing a relationship with the natural world and using magic to help yourself and others. You can work magic to gain more control over your life – to start making it go the way you want, rather than leaving things to chance. You can use it for healing, to create opportunities, or to foster friendships. Use it for anything you want – so long as it harms no one.

Above Anyone can be a witch today and many practising are about as ordinary looking as the girl next door.

Left A mirror symbolizes psychic powers and is a common tool used by witches for divination.

The basics

Before you start flicking the pages and looking for the

spells, there are a few things you should know first

about white witchcraft in general, and about how to

prepare yourself for spellweaving.

*...what every
self-respecting
witch needs
to know...*

This section will give you a good grounding of

the rudimentary basics. The first few pages will provide

an informative insight into what witches believe. You

will learn about the witch's belief in

the power of nature and our links

with the cosmos, and how the

changing seasons of the year and

the patterns of the stars and

planets influence our life on earth.

The traditions behind the witch's

annual festivals are explained, and how to work with

the powers of the moon, the sun and the four elements

throughout the year. You will also learn useful and

...the power of nature and our links with the cosmos...

practical information about the

witch's tool kit, where and when

it is best to spellweave, and

about the

preparation

rituals that

you need to

follow prior to working a spell. And

lastly, don't miss the special pages

on meditation, scrying and inner

journeys; all very useful further

knowledge to help you on your

path to practising white witchcraft.

It's weird!

You probably don't realize this but when we use the word "weird" we are acknowledging the existence of uncanny, supernatural powers. The word comes from the Anglo-Saxon "Wyrd", which people thought of as an all-powerful sense of destiny that shapes the world. It can be imagined as a magical web in which all of life is interconnected.

Above We are all part of a giant web of life, and white magic seeks to tap into its hidden forces to cause positive change.

the web of life

White witches believe that we are part of the Wyrd or "web of life", intimately connected to all things and one another via invisible forces and energies. These energies radiate from everything in the universe – from the moon and stars in the heavens to rocks and stones on earth, sending out subtle vibrations along invisible energy pathways.

The art of white magic is about tuning in to these "vibes" and working with the natural and elemental ingredients of the universe to bring about positive change. These "ingredients" include the planets, light, colour, crystals, gems, birds, animals, trees and plants.

Everything in the natural world has unique properties that can be used for making spells and charms. Part of a witch's training is to build up a repertoire of mystical knowledge based on this natural information.

Above White magic is about working positively with the energies of the natural world and the use of tree magic is prominent in many spells.

witches and nature

Witches believe that it is important for us to live in harmony with the natural world as this affects our health and happiness on every level, mentally, emotionally and spiritually. What we think, how we feel and what we aspire to are intrinsically linked to the world around us, as part of the web of life. White witches "tread lightly on the earth" and honour nature's bounty for supplying us with everything that we need – food, warmth and shelter. More importantly though, witches make use of nature's gifts for making positive magic through spellweaving.

Left Seashells are one of nature's many ingredients with unseen energies from the ocean that one can tune into through white witching.

stones and crystals

Stones, crystals and gems are used extensively in white magic. Select the ones that have particular meaning for your spellweaving.

• agate	inspiration from the spiritual realms
• amethyst	mental and spiritual balance
• aquamarine	increase psychic powers
• citrine	wealth and prosperity
• celestite	link with angels
• flint	psychic protection
• fossil	link with earth wisdom
• malachite	releases deep hurts and resentments and breaks ties
• moss agate	earth healing
• seashell	fertility
• smoky quartz	absorbs negative vibes, grounds and stabilizes
• tiger's eye	speeds up energy flow
• turquoise	healing and protection
• vanadinite	mental focus, life direction

trees

Like everything else in nature, trees also have special qualities. Work with a particular tree according to the type of spell you are weaving.

• ash, aspen, elder, eucalyptus	healing
• alder, bamboo, pine, witch hazel, yew	spiritual
• bay, birch, broom, cedar, tamarisk, willow	purification
• ash, cypress, holly, larch, mulberry, rowan, oak	protection
• banana, birch, fig, hazelnut, oak, pine (cones), walnut, willow	fertility
• apple, ash, hazel, rowan, willow, witch hazel	enhancing magic
• apple, apricot, pomegranate, nut, willow	love
• alder, almond, bamboo, horse chestnut, pine, witch hazel, yew	prosperity

feathers

Feathers have many different meanings, depending on which bird they come from. When you are outside, look out for any fallen feathers and keep them for your spellweaving.

• blackbird	gatekeeper
• crow	change
• duck	love and harmony
• eagle	clarity
• hawk	foresight
• magpie	relationships
• owl	wisdom
• pigeon	messages
• robin	protection
• swan	purity
• woodpecker	magic and prophecy
• wren	protection

what's in a spell?

A spell is very simple. It is a positive affirmation, using focused energy. Our universe has abundant energy which you can use for the good. In learning how to work positively with the elements, animals, trees, minerals, planets and stars, you can build your own magical bridge upon which you can walk quite safely, because all things are energetically connected.

In weaving a spell, what you ask for is what you'll receive, so be realistic with your request. Fame, riches and issues of control are best left alone as they move away from positive magic. An important aspect of spellweaving is effort: the amount of energy you put in sets the energetic scene for the spell itself.

Left Witches see all of nature as part of a pattern of the universe and have a great love and respect for all creation.

The wheel of the year

Different regions of the world have different seasonal and directional patterns, but the sabbats can be celebrated anywhere following the seasons, rather than the specific dates given.

To a witch, the cycles of nature show that life is a never-ending journey of birth, growth, death and rebirth. This journey is represented by the wheel of the year, which is divided into eight festivals or sabbats. Four of the sabbats are solar festivals while the other four are Celtic in origin. By celebrating the sabbats, you place yourself at the centre of the wheel and an active role in life.

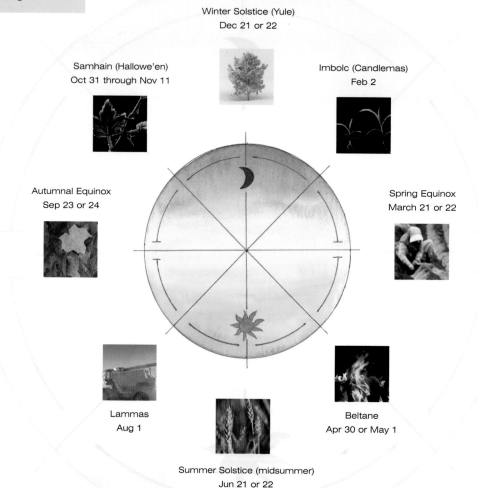

Winter Solstice (Yule)
Dec 21 or 22

Samhain (Hallowe'en)
Oct 31 through Nov 11

Imbolc (Candlemas)
Feb 2

Autumnal Equinox
Sep 23 or 24

Spring Equinox
March 21 or 22

Lammas
Aug 1

Beltane
Apr 30 or May 1

Summer Solstice (midsummer)
Jun 21 or 22

the eight sabbats

The word "sabbat" in French means "to celebrate". Witches hold these celebrations to mark important turning points of the year, using the energies of the changing seasons for peace, prosperity, health and good luck. Sabbats are normally celebrated with feasting and rituals. The celebrations usually last from sunset until sunset the next day.

Winter Solstice (Yule)
This is the shortest day of the year. The sun is at its lowest point and night overshadows day. The moon's power is at its strongest. It is a time of feasting, to celebrate the rebirth of the sun, which will begin its ascent through the skies, dispelling darkness and bringing life to earth.
★ Custom: putting up a holly wreath to symbolize the wheel of the year.
★ Best action: time to give gifts, relax and celebrate.

Imbolc (Candlemas)
The word "imbolc" means "ewe's milk" in Celtic and it is the time of new beginnings. The first green shoots appear, and it is the start of the lambing season. It is a time of hope as the days begin to get longer and the hours of darkness shorter.
★ Custom: lighting candles to celebrate the return of the light.
★ Best action: make plans and lay the foundations for the future, such as planning a job or house move.

Spring Equinox
The sun increases in power and night and day are equal. Return of fertility to the land and a time of great energy as the life force gathers strength and the sap rises.
★ Custom: planting the first seeds.
★ Best action: "spring cleaning" – throw out your junk to make way for the new; include clearing up any outstanding negative acts or thoughts and start with a clean slate; don't put things off; use the energy of spring to your advantage and take action.

Beltane
The word "beltane" means "bright fire" in Gaelic and is the festival of light and life. It heralds the first day of summer and was traditionally marked by the lighting of bonfires to symbolize the strength of the rising sun.
★ Custom: May Day festivals; maypole dancing, fertility rites.
★ Best action: take part in creative projects or enjoy the company of friends; a good time for fertility magic.

Summer Solstice (midsummer)
The longest day is celebrated at summer solstice, a time marked by the stones of many of Europe's ancient monuments. The sun is at its greatest power and the fruits ripen.
★ Custom: healing herbs are harvested.
★ Best action: a good time to be dynamic and active; use magic to help with material matters, such as jobs, houses or money, or to help bring romance into your life.

Lammas
Traditionally, Lammas (or "loaf mass" in Celtic) was a time when the first new grain was baked into bread. This festival celebrates the giving of thanks to nature for all her fruits, a time of reaping what has been sown.
★ Custom: the harvesting of grains and medicinal plants.
★ Best action: take time to reflect on your life and "count your blessings"; be grateful for what you have.

Autumnal Equinox
The wheel of the year is turning and the sun's power is diminishing, giving way to the power of the moon. We are reminded of the cold, dark months ahead.
★ Custom: gathering of orchard fruits and later harvests.
★ Best action: examine your life and prune it of all non-essential activities; prepare to turn your attention inwards by studying, reading or spending more time indoors; a good time to start developing magical powers.

Samhain (Hallowe'en)
Also known as the "Witch's New Year", Samhain marks the end of summer and the start of winter. It is a time when the veil between past, present and future is thin and it is possible to see beyond into the "otherworld".
★ Custom: divination to seek guidance and a new direction for the coming season; sharing legends and stories.
★ Best action: look back over your life and see how your past has shaped the present; see what it is that is holding you back and let go.

Right Samhain or Hallowe'en is the largest celebration of the wheel of the year and witches often decorate their altars with pumpkins and other fare related to the season.

The sun and the moon

White witches work with the energies of the sun and the moon. The sun is the bringer of life, and makes us feel optimistic, happy and healthy. The moon is powerful and mysterious, influencing not only the tides and the weather, but also our moods and behaviour. The sun is linked with masculine energy and the moon with feminine powers.

Above Use the sun's healing force and simply pick a spot where its rays can bathe you.

solar power

The sun is an immense fireball of light and heat, and its beaming rays influence our health and vitality. Too little sunlight can make you feel tired and depressed, and when someone is ill it is as though his or her "light" has dimmed. Observing the path of the sun through the year and celebrating the sabbats around The Wheel of the Year (p12-13) is one way of working with the sun's energies. Eating natural sun-ripened food is another, or you can also try using "sunny" colours such as oranges, yellows and reds in your clothing or surroundings.

If you are feeling depressed or unwell, relax in a sunny spot outside and let sunlight wash all over your body. Feel the brilliant white-gold rays soaking into your skin and driving out the darkness of disease. If it is cold and grey outside, you can also do this using your imaginative powers: find a spot where you feel warm and relaxed, and as you breathe in, see your body infused with golden sunlight; as you breathe out, see the darkness leaving your body.

Below In many traditions the sun was worshipped for its healing powers. Witches take the light of the sun into account when working magic.

lunar power

The moon is most strongly associated with the imagination and with psychic, intuitive powers. The moon has four phases: waxing, full, waning and dark. Witches observe the phases of the moon and time their spells in accordance with its cycle.

Above The waxing moon heralds the beginning of a new cycle, and is the time in magic when new opportunities can be called for.

the first phase: waxing moon (new)
★ East wind.
★ Timing: beginning of a new cycle; development and growth; new opportunities.
★ Lesson: to invoke – knowing.
★ Work on: personal issues and put plans into action for the month ahead.

the second phase: full moon
★ South wind.
★ Timing: the moon is full and ripe; a very fertile time but care is needed as the energies are so powerful.
★ Lesson: to expand – manifesting.
★ Work on: increase and expansion in your day to day affairs; a good time for personal power and magnetism.

the third phase: waning moon (old)
★ West wind.
★ Timing: the moon's power is decreasing; release and letting go.
★ Lesson: to let go – courage.

★ Work on: letting go of the past; a powerful time for healing. It is also the time for insights and increasing psychic power.

the fourth phase: dark moon (no moon)
★ North wind.
★ Timing: the moon disappears; time for retreat and withdrawal, to recharge energies before the cycle starts again.
★ Lesson: to learn – to keep silence.
★ Work on: gaining wisdom, understanding, insight. This time is best spent in contemplation, meditation and preparation, or seeking guidance. White witches do not work spells at this time.

the blue moon
About every two or three years, two full moons occur in the same calendar month. This is known as a "blue moon" and is a rare but special time as the moon's powers are doubled during that month.
★ Use the blue moon to set long-term objectives, to sow seeds for the future, giving them time to germinate and grow.
★ Extra caution is needed now as your wish and intent will be doubled in power.

moon-dreaming

The practice of magic involves working with the subconscious, irrational, intuitive side of the psyche. It is a good idea to get used to working with dreams as that will help to develop this aspect of you, making it easier to visualize and spellweave when you are awake.

Before you go to sleep, tell yourself that you want to remember your dreams and start to keep a dream diary, writing your dreams down when you wake. Even if you can't remember the whole dream, or it doesn't seem to make any sense, record as much as you can – it is good practice and will start to sharpen your psychic and intuitive powers.

Esbats

Lunar festivals are called "esbats" and are held on the first night of the full moon. They are times of celebration and power. Requests and dedications are made and a feast shared to honour the moon's mother aspect of great abundance and fertility.

Above By sharpening our access to dreamtime we hone our psychic powers.

Elemental energies

The universe is made up of the four elements – air, fire, water and earth. Life is a balance between these forces, both as energies in the outer world and within every human being. When weaving spells and charms, witches work with these elemental energies, each of which has certain characteristics and symbolic correspondences.

Above Water covers over two-thirds of the earth's surface and corresponds with our own body mass which is two-thirds water.

air

Air is invisible but all around you. It is associated with scudding clouds and the open spaces of the heavenly sky, and symbolizes freedom and movement. Its direction is east where the sun rises, and its season is spring when the winds blow, bringing change and new beginnings. Work with the air element to start projects, for travel, study and learning, and anything associated with communication. When air is out of balance it means that things are "airy fairy" and there is a danger that plans never become real. It can be a tricky element to work with as its nature is not to be pinned down.

fire

Fire is the spark of life. Its direction is south and its season is high summer when the sun is at its strongest, bringing warmth and ripening the crops. The sabbats Imbolc, Beltane, Lammas and Samhain are all fire festivals, called "days of power" by some witches. Fire is associated with intuition, creativity, fertility, sexuality and passion. Work with the fire element for good luck, romance, making friends and socializing. Use it when enthusiasm, ambition, risk-taking or an extra push of energy is needed. When fire is out of balance it warms the blood and leads to hot tempers and arguments and a tendency to be reckless. There is also a danger of going to excess and suffering burn-out.

water

More than two-thirds of the earth's surface is covered in water, and our bodies are also largely made up of this element. Water is the elixir of life and has healing and rejuvenating properties. Its direction is west where the sun sets, and its season is autumn when the power of the sun gives way to the rising moon. It is associated with feelings and emotions. Work with the water element for healing and to increase psychic sensitivity – water soaks up atmospheres and quickly senses the vibe in any situation. Too much water is the "wet blanket", who dampens everyone's spirits, or a "doormat" who can't stand up for themselves.

earth

Earth contains all the elements. It is the element that brings things together and symbolizes the physical body and all the good things of life. It is the "Earth Mother" that nurtures and protects us all. Its direction is north and its time is winter when the sun is weakest and the moon is strongest. Earth is associated with stability, cohesion and the power to manifest in the material world. Work with the earth element in business or career matters, to create prosperity and abundance, and where inner strength, stamina and patience are called for. Too much earth leads to being a "stick-in-the-mud", in danger of getting stuck in routine habits, or of over-indulging in physical pleasures, which can create health problems.

the elemental energies and their correspondences

Air
- ★ Symbolizes: intellect, rational thought, mental agility
- ★ Direction: east
- ★ Magical symbol: sword, dagger or feather
- ★ Time and season: sunrise/spring

Fire
- ★ Symbolizes: creativity, ambition, passion, intuition
- ★ Direction: south
- ★ Magical symbol: wand, candle or flame
- ★ Time and season: midday/summer

Water
- ★ Symbolizes: feelings, emotional world, psychic sensitivity
- ★ Direction: west
- ★ Magical symbol: chalice or bowl of water
- ★ Time and season: evening/autumn

Earth
- ★ Symbolizes: physical body, stability, cohesion, manifestation, money, material goods
- ★ Direction: north
- ★ Magical symbol: pentacle, salt or stone
- ★ Time and season: night/winter

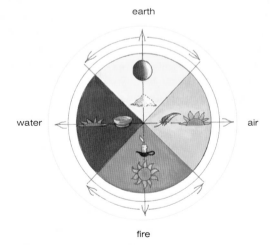

earth

water

air

fire

the pentacle and the five elements

The pentacle or pentagram is a five-pointed star, point up, enclosed by a circle. It symbolizes the human form (the legs are represented by the bottom points of the star, the arms by the points to the left and right, the head by the top point of the star) enclosed in the eternal circle of "spirit" or life. The five points also represent the "five" elements – air, fire, water and earth plus "ether" (or spirit), the fifth element. This is the traditional magical symbol used by witches.

the guardian angels

The elements are also associated with the angels that guard the four directions. Each angel is a messenger of God and has special powers. If you don't believe in God, you can think of this as the "healing spirit of the universe", or the god (good) force. It is common to invoke the angels for their help and protection when casting a spell. Their names are pronounced in separate syllables, for example, Michael is spoken as Mik-i-el. The "el" part of any angelic name means "god" (or good).

Raphael (Helper of God)
- ★ Appearance: clothed in pale blues and whites of the sky, or the yellow and peaches of sunrise.
- ★ Element: air
- ★ Direction: east

Michael (Like unto God)
- ★ Appearance: wears scarlet robes and gold armour. He carries a sword with a flame-shaped blade.
- ★ Element: fire
- ★ Direction: south

Gabriel (Strength of God)
- ★ Appearance: carries a great chalice or Grail, and wears silver, blues and sea-green robes.
- ★ Element: water
- ★ Direction: west

Uriel (Light of God)
- ★ Appearance: robed in the colours of the seasons – black, brown, green and the gold of ripe corn.
- ★ Element: earth
- ★ Direction: north

Signs of the zodiac

In western astrology there are twelve signs of the zodiac. Each sign has a planetary ruler and is governed by one of the four elements. The moon travels through these constellations approximately every 27-28 days, whereas the sun takes a year. The dates shown for each sign refer to the approximate time when the sun is in that sign. To find out when the moon is in a particular sign, you would need to refer to a book of planetary tables called an "ephemeris".

the stars and planets

There is a right time and purpose for everything. Before the advent of clocks and calendars, people measured time by the patterns of movement in the starry night sky. These patterns form the constellations of the zodiac, each of which has symbolic associations that can be used to influence the best timing for spells.

Aries (21 Mar – 19 Apr)

Element: fire
Planetary ruler: Mars
Spells for: business, success, innovation, leadership, self-assertion

Taurus (20 Apr – 20 May)

Element: earth
Planetary ruler: Venus
Spells for: material matters, nourishment, physical health, love

Gemini (21 May – 21 Jun)

Element: air
Planetary ruler: Mercury
Spells for: communication, travel, learning, study

Cancer (22 Jun – 22 Jul)

Element: water
Planetary ruler: Moon
Spells for: family, friends, emotional health, the home, motherhood

Leo (23 July – 22 Aug)

Element: fire
Planetary ruler: Sun
Spells for: success, wealth, recognition, vitality and wellbeing

Virgo (23 Aug – 22 Sep)

Element: earth
Planetary ruler: Mercury
Spells for: harvest, abundance, fruitfulness

Libra (23 Sep – 23 Oct)

Element: air
Planetary ruler: Venus
Spells for: balance, harmony, relationships, partnerships

Scorpio (24 Oct – 21 Nov)

Element: water
Planetary ruler: Pluto
Spells for: sexuality, ancestors, spiritual understanding, insight

Sagittarius (22 Nov – 21 Dec)

Element: fire
Planetary ruler: Jupiter
Spells for: travel, expansion, transcendence, wisdom

Capricorn (22 Dec – 19 Jan)

Element: earth
Planetary ruler: Saturn
Spells for: material matters and concerns, obstacles, challenges

Aquarius (20 Jan – 18 Feb)

Element: air
Planetary ruler: Uranus
Spells for: healing, higher thought, mental health, freedom

Pisces (19 Feb – 20 Mar)

Element: water
Planetary ruler: Neptune
Spells for: psychic work, creative ideas, dreams, healing

the planets and the days and hours of the week

Each day is associated with a planet and can be dedicated to a particular kind of magic. There are also magical hours dedicated to each planet. They are not clock hours but one-twelfth of the time between local sunrise and sunset, and sunset and sunrise. The first hour of each day from sunrise is dedicated to the planet whose day it is, and the following hours are ruled by the planets in this rolling sequence: Moon, Saturn, Jupiter, Mars, Sun, Venus, Mercury then Moon, Saturn, etc.

Sunday
A day for solar magic. Work on personal healing or for a new impulse to assist your life. Spellweave to attract health, success and prosperity.
- ★ Planet: Sun
- ★ Colour: gold, yellow
- ★ Number: 6
- ★ Incense: cedar, frankincense
- ★ Mineral: gold, topaz, amber
- ★ Herb: cinnamon, bay
- ★ Tree: birch

Monday
Use the silvery light of the Moon to strengthen psychic or dreaming powers. Spellweave to increase intuition, perceptions, fertility and for all female issues.
- ★ Planet: Moon
- ★ Colour: silver/white
- ★ Number: 9
- ★ Incense: jasmine, sandalwood
- ★ Mineral: pearl, moonstone, silver
- ★ Herb: eucalyptus
- ★ Tree: willow

Tuesday
Use the fiery energy of Mars to kick-start yourself into action. Spellweave to improve strength, power and authority, and to banish conflicts.
- ★ Planet: Mars (Tiw in Saxon)
- ★ Colour: red
- ★ Number: 9
- ★ Incense: tobacco, pine
- ★ Mineral: iron, haematite, ruby
- ★ Herb: coriander (cilantro), garlic, pepper
- ★ Tree: holly

Wednesday
Mercury highlights interaction and travel. Spellweave for all forms of communication.
- ★ Planet: Mercury (Wotan in Saxon)
- ★ Colour: orange, yellow
- ★ Number: 8
- ★ Incense: mastic
- ★ Mineral: agate, carnelian, quicksilver
- ★ Herb: caraway, lavender, marjoram, dill
- ★ Tree: ash

Thursday
Jupiter rules over business, material growth, justice and legal matters. Spellweave for job opportunities, luck, travel and money.
- ★ Planet: Jupiter (Thor in Saxon)
- ★ Colour: royal blue, violet, purple
- ★ Number: 4
- ★ Incense: cedar wood
- ★ Mineral: amethyst, aquamarine, tin
- ★ Herb: nutmeg, sage, anise, cloves
- ★ Tree: oak

Friday
Venus is the goddess of love and harmony and rules over all kinds of partnerships. Spellweave for love, friendship, marriage, beauty and creativity.
- ★ Planet: Venus (Freya in Saxon)
- ★ Colour: green
- ★ Number: 7
- ★ Incense: rose, patchouli
- ★ Mineral: emerald, jade, copper
- ★ Herb: vervain, myrtle, yarrow
- ★ Tree: apple

Saturday
Father of the gods and ruler of time, Saturn's magic is slow and gentle but very powerful. Spellweave to remove obstacles and restrictions.
- ★ Planet: Saturn
- ★ Colour: black, indigo
- ★ Number: 3
- ★ Incense: myrrh, cypress
- ★ Mineral: jet, obsidian, lead, pewter
- ★ Herb: asafoetida
- ★ Tree: alder

The witch's tool kit

The equipment and materials that are needed for weaving magic are easy to find. Start to build up a store of magical ingredients, keeping your eye out for stones, crystals, feathers and unusual bits and pieces such as pieces of driftwood or coloured glass.

making a wand

you will need

- piece of wood about 1.5cm (2/3in) thick and about 1m (1yd) long
- selection of paints, including bright rainbow colours and black and white
- thin card
- glue

1 Paint a wide white band at the top of the wooden stick and paint the other end of the shaft black.

2 Between the white and black, paint 12 coloured bands starting with scarlet, then orange, yellow, green and blue etc.

3 While the paint is drying make the water lily for the top by cutting the card into three flower shapes and decorating it with colour. When dry, glue the flower onto the end of the wand.

wand

A wand is probably the most well-known item in the witch's tool kit. It is a pointer that is used to channel energy, directing your will out-wards. Wands can be used to cast the circle and to make invocations. They can be made from a simple twig or piece of wood, which you can carve and decorate as you like.

candles

Whether it's on an altar or in a magic circle, candles are used to light the sacred space. Different coloured candles are chosen according to the type of spell you are working.
- ★ Romance – shocking pink, red
- ★ Friendship – all shades of pink
- ★ Prosperity – green, gold, orange
- ★ Healing – yellow, green, pink
- ★ Protection – black, all shades of blue
- ★ Peace – cream
- ★ Psychic powers – silver, blue, purple

white cord

The cord is used for casting the magic circle. A piece that is 2.7m (9ft) long and about 5mm (1/4in) thick is ideal.

salt

Witches use salt is used for cleansing and purification. At the end of your spellweaving, the salt should be sprinkled or buried in the earth, but make sure you choose a spot where it will not damage any plant life.

natural paper and pens

Many spells involve writing, so choose a good-quality, natural paper. Gold and silver represent the energies of the sun and the moon respectively.

incense

For thousands of years incense has been used in ritual and ceremony for thousands of years to cleanse and purify the atmosphere, and to invoke the gods. It is available as sticks or loose. Loose incense has a much better smell and can be burned in a charcoal burner, widely available in many stores. Materials that you have dried yourself, such as resin from

Left A candle in a cauldron is used to represent the element of fire in spells.

Above Incense is a vital part of white witching with different types used for different spells.

★ Bay: protection, psychic powers
★ Cinnamon: spirituality, healing, psychic powers, love
★ Garlic: protection, healing
★ Ginger: love, money, success
★ Eucalyptus: healing, protection
★ Jasmine: aphrodisiac, love, stimulates imagination
★ Lavender: longevity, health, protection
★ Thyme: psychic powers, protection, courage
★ Vanilla: sharpening mental powers
★ Rosemary: protection, love, youth
★ Sage: wisdom, longevity
★ Peppermint: purification
★ Orange: luck, divination, money

stones, rocks and crystals

Many spells call for a stone or crystal, which can absorb, transform and transmit energy. Start to build up a collection, choosing the stones that you feel most drawn to – this can be anything from a beautiful amethyst point to a polished pebble on the beach. Always keep your stones clean – regularly bathing them in salt water at the time of the full moon helps to cleanse them of negative energies.

spellbags

Many spells also need a spellbag or drawstring pouch. You can buy spell-bags ready made in New Age shops or stores selling handmade goods from around the world, or else you can make your own.

pine trees, or wood shavings from apple, pine or other trees can also be added. The stems of many culinary herbs, including rosemary, sage or fennel, burn quite well if they are dry.
★ Frankincense: connection to higher powers, protection
★ Sandalwood: aids meditation, purification, cutting ties with the past
★ Myrrh: awareness of mysteries of life, dispels fear

herbs and essential oils

Herbs and plant oils are also used in magic. Every plant has unique qualities that can be transmitted to us via our sense of smell, and used for a particular purpose. Essential oils may be burned in a room vaporizer, or add a few drops to your spellmaking equipment. Herbs are used in charms and dried herbs can be added to your incense mix.

Above Stones and crystals are highly prized for their healing and spiritual properties as well as their beauty.

Countdown to magic

For successful spellweaving adequate preparation is most important. Putting in the effort during the initial stages will set the energetic scene for the spell itself. It is worth finding the time to track down all the correct ingredients, and also to prepare yourself, so that you are in the right frame of mind for making magic.

Above The flame of a candle is a valuable symbol of light in spellweaving, and also represents the south wind – the wind of summer.

preparation rituals

Do not work a spell if you feel tired, or drained of energy, and/or when your mind is busy. Begin by taking a shower and putting on fresh clothes – some people like to have clothes worn only when making magic. Wear clothes that do not constrict the flow of energy through your body – loose-fitting trousers (pants) and a top, or a full-length robe are ideal, preferably in a natural fabric. It is best to be barefoot so that your feet can connect with the earth. Another form of cleansing is called smudging and uses smoke from burning sage leaves, frankincense or juniper aromatherapy oil.

golden light breathing

This simple exercise will help to "change your energy" and put you in the right space for spellweaving. It is a cleansing and empowering technique that increases energy in the body, giving you more resources to work with. It is a good idea to use it when you are weaving a difficult spell that you need all your powers for.

1 Stand with your feet hip-width apart and feel them make contact with the ground. Rest your hands on your stomach and take a few deep breaths into the stomach area.

2 Place both hands just below the sternum. Begin to breathe, not too deeply, but slowly and with concentration.

3 Breathe in through the nose and visualize drawing golden light into yourself. Hold the breath for a short time (do not strain) and imagine your heart opening. Breathe out through the mouth, letting the golden light circulate around your body as you do so.

4 Keep doing this breathing until you feel energized and wide awake. Then rest your hands on your heart for a few moments, letting the breath return to normal.

Right Cleansing yourself with smoke is called smudging. Dried sage leaves are placed in a heat-proof bowl and lit, then a feather is used to fan the cleansing smoke around the body.

spellweaver's pledge

Remember that what you give out in magic returns to you threefold, so it is important to make sure you are always working from the "right place". The spellweaver's pledge is done from the heart, and aligns your intention to goodness and light. You should always perform it before making magic.

1 Place your hands on your heart and ask that you be filled with the light of love. Imagine golden light and feelings of love filling your heart and then your whole body.

2 Let the light begin to radiate out in all directions around you, so that you are surrounded by a golden aura of love.

3 Open your arms and raise them above your head, palms facing up towards the heavens, and say the pledge. Then bring your arms down to your sides and say:

I call upon the divine will of the universe to send a blessing upon my heart, so that I may be filled with the light of love and truth in all that I do. I pledge that from this day, I will do my best to harm none with my thoughts, words, or deeds. I pledge that any magic I perform will be for the highest good of all. And so may it be!

blessing equipment

All equipment that you intend to use for spellweaving should be cleansed and consecrated first. For the purpose of this example, we will imagine that the cord is being blessed.

you will need
compass
incense
candle
bowl of spring water
bowl of sea salt
cord

1 In a cleared space outside or on the floor, mark out a circle with the four points of the compass. Put the incense in the east, the candle in the south, the bowl of water in the west and the bowl of salt in the north.

2 Beginning with the east, light the incense and say while passing your ingredients through the smoke:

I cleanse, bless and consecrate this cord with the powers of air.

3 Repeat this through the south, west and north quarters, passing the cord through the candle flame, and sprinkling it with water and salt respectively. Each time repeat the blessing statement, changing "powers of air" to "powers of fire", "powers of water" and "powers of earth" respectively.

4 Finish by saying:

May this cord now be cleansed and purified for the highest good of all. And so may it be!

the power of three

Before you begin sending wishes and casting spells, remember that what you give out in magic returns to you threefold. The energy you put into your spells increases and grows as it is released, so exercise caution and prudence with what you wish for. Always ask with sincerity, from the heart and thereby from the true power that you hold within. Do not fear magic, but instead learn how to be humble and how to ask for things in the right way.

Sacred space

Each time you cast a spell you need to create a special space in which to work. This space is the magic or sacred circle, and is always arranged according to the cardinal points of north, south, east and west. It should always be closed before and after the spell. If you are working with other helpers, such as angels or totem animals, use their names instead in the greeting.

alternative circles

You do not always have to use a cord to cast your circle. You can use other objects such as tealight candles or stones for instance, or even use your wand to draw an invisible circle. Always bless the materials first.

casting the circle

The circle is a symbol of wholeness and should be cast in a clockwise ("deosil") direction. Working within the sacred circle keeps the world outside at bay and contains your energy. Do not step out until you have finished.

you will need
2.7m (9ft) white cord
bowl of salt water

1 Place the cord in an opened circle upon the ground, with the opening in the east. Step through the opening with your spell ingredients and place them in the centre.

2 Close the circle behind you and seal it with a sprinkling of salt water.

3 Go deosil around the circle, sprinkling salt water on the cord. Visualize yourself surrounded by golden light. Hold your right arm out, follow your cord circle deosil with your finger and say the light invocation:

By the powers of Heaven and Earth, I cast this circle in the name of love, light, wisdom and truth for the highest good of all. And so may it be!

You are now ready to weave your chosen spell.

closing the circle

Closing the circle is as important as opening it – it keeps the spell-working energy contained and "clean". It is done by working anticlockwise ("widdershins") until you end up where you started your spell. For instance, if you started working your spell in the south, you would close by beginning in the east and moving round through north and west until you reach the south. As you go round, gather up your ingredients from each quarter and say:

I give thanks to all who have helped me and leave my request with you. And so may it be.

When you have finished, make an opening in the circle and put all the materials outside. Any organic ingredients (such as water and salt for instance) should be safely recycled in the earth.

making an offering

Making magic is a give-and-take relationship. When casting spells, it is important to give thanks to your unseen helpers and the spirit or energies of any equipment that you use or the place that you visit or work from. Making an offering is a way of acknowledging them and encourages their co-operation.

you will need
2.7m (9ft) white cord
feather
red candle
bowl of water
salt

1 Make a cord circle as before. Take the feather in your right hand and hold it first to your heart and then out to the east.

2 Say the dedication:

Hail to thee East Wind. I ask permission to work with your energies and call for your blessing upon this ceremony. I make this offering to you.

Place the feather just inside your cord circle, in the east.

3 Place the candle in the south and light it, repeating the dedication, this time to the South Wind.

4 Continue with the offerings of water for the west and salt for the north, repeating the dedication each time. When you have finished, stand still for a few moments and then gather up your offerings and cord.

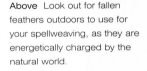

Above Look out for fallen feathers outdoors to use for your spellweaving, as they are energetically charged by the natural world.

golden rules for white witches

★ Work from the heart and do what you do with gentleness and responsibility.

★ Seek no revenge and send no ill will – for whatever you send will return to you.

★ Remember it is illegal to pick wild flowers or disturb protected species.

★ When using herbs and flowers always work with petals or leaves in numbers of three, seven or nine.

★ Do not manipulate the free will of another or control events to suit yourself.

★ If you wish to undo a spell, light a white candle and some frankincense. Burn the written-down spell in the candle flame and say "This spell is undone. So be it."

★ Always include the words "for the highest good of all" in a spell to insure against negative influence.

★ Keep yourself, your working space and equipment clean and free of psychic dirt.

Meditation

When making magic, it is important to be as relaxed and free in body, mind and spirit as possible. Meditation is a powerful tool that promotes deep relaxation in all areas of your being, slowing down the brain waves into a relaxed alpha pattern similar to deep sleep.

Above Running can be an active form of meditation, not to mention good for your health.

active meditation

There are countless ways to meditate, some active, some passive. What is important is to find a method that works for you and to practise it regularly, particularly when you are about to spellweave.

Meditation is the quality of awareness that we bring to an act. It is about raising our levels of consciousness so that we are aware of our activity and of any thoughts and emotions that we are experiencing in the moment as we do it. In which case, any act can become a meditation; it is a question of bringing our notice to what we are doing. If you enjoy walking, for instance, you can make this your meditation. Instead of hurriedly rushing to be somewhere, slow down and take the time to feel your feet connect with the earth as you take each step. As you walk, be mindful of what you are doing, thinking and feeling, and be aware of your energy flowing through your body.

Above Create your own little meditation sanctuary indoors, using veils to shield you from the world.

passive meditation

Meditation is about relaxing and letting go into deeper levels of our being, and sometimes this is best achieved through passive "non-doing" states. Bringing awareness to the breath is a good way of bringing attention into the "here-and-now", using each out-breath to relax a little more deeply. Many meditation practices involve working with the breath in a sitting or lying down position, as the mind and body can most easily unwind in these positions.

Right Any act can be meditative, including simply seeking out your favourite spot outside for a quiet period of contemplation and to connect with the earth.

lying down meditation

1 Lie down on the floor, with something soft, such as a blanket or rug, beneath your back. Lie relaxed with your hands by your sides. Close your eyes, concentrate and try to feel your body. Notice which parts feel slightly tense and which feel completely relaxed.

2 Start with your toes. Breathing in, clench them up as hard as you can and then as you breathe out, release them. Next, do the same with your ankles. As you breathe in, tense them to bring your feet off the floor and then relax as you breathe out.

3 Work your way slowly up your body, clenching and relaxing your knees, your thighs, your bottom, your stomach, your fingers, hands, wrists, arms and your shoulders, all the way up to your head. Finally, try to clench the scalp of your head and then relax it. Take a long, slow breath, and relax, breathing out. Notice your body again. If there are any parts that still feel a little tense, repeat the exercise with them.

4 When your whole body is relaxed, lie completely still with your eyes closed and let your breathing find its own rhythm. Lie in this position for about 10 minutes, and then start to bring a little movement back into your hands and feet, arms and legs. Have a good yawn and a stretch, open your eyes and return to normal waking consciousness.

dance meditation

If you enjoy dancing, make it a meditation. Find a place where you won't be disturbed and put on some music that you enjoy to dance to. Experiment with moving different parts of your body. Start by dancing with the head and neck, then with the shoulders. Bring in your arms, elbows, wrists and fingertips so that your whole upper body is in motion. Then introduce the movement of the spine, the sway of your hips, and the thousand ways to move your legs and feet, even your toes. If you cannot move some parts of your body, move as much as you are able to. Do not be self-conscious: this dance is not for anyone else but you. Just let your whole body express your feelings with the music, becoming comfortable with every pore of your body speaking your heart.

Above A classic meditative pose. Linking thumbs and index fingers allows energy to continuously circulate instead of flowing away.

Scrying

Scrying is the art of divining by seeing pictures in a crystal ball, pool of water or other reflective surface. To scry, you need to reach an altered state of consciousness but then work with open eyes. It is quite tricky to achieve, and takes time, practice and concentration.

tips for developing scrying skills

★ Practise working with dream recall, as scrying uses a very similar type of inner vision.

★ Don't try too hard; relaxation is the key.

★ Watch without trying to "grab hold of" the material you see before you; let it float past your vision like a film reel.

★ Scrying within a circle of light will help to keep the outside world and its distractions at bay.

Right A calm, natural pool in tranquil surroundings can make an excellent medium for scrying.

finding your relaxed state

The first step in scrying is learning how to enter a space of deep relaxation at will. Find a quiet spot and sit upright with your feet on the floor and arms relaxed. Close your eyes and breathe out fully. At your own speed, breathe in for a count of four; hold the breath for a count of four; breathe out for a count of four; and hold your breath out for a count of four. Repeat this entire sequence at least 10 times. If you lose count, start again from the beginning. If this pattern is too hard, try a slower 10-5-10-5 pattern. Your whole attention should be focused on breathing rhythmically and relaxing physically; gradually, this will help you to become calm and focused.

learning to scry

1 Allow yourself to sink into a relaxed state and then gently open your eyes, holding them in soft focus, to regard the crystal ball.

2 Forming the question in your mind, look "into" the glass. You may find that the glass becomes cloudy or dim initially, and a dark patch may appear through the "mist".

3 Continue looking, keeping the eyes relaxed and softly focused, the breathing gentle and easy. You might find that pictures, signs, numbers, words or other symbols may appear before you. This may not happen at first, but will come with regular practice.

Inner journeys

Above Visualize your path into inner knowledge as like the inner vortex of a seashell.

The path of the white witch is about bringing inner knowledge to bear on the world outside. A vivid imagination, directed by magical training, is the most effective tool we have for changing the world. It is something that has often lain dormant since childhood, but we can work with it in creative ways to reawaken its power.

inner journey exercise

Here is a basic inner journey exercise. Picture the journey in as much detail and as clearly as you can, paying attention to images, feelings, smells and other perceptions along the way. Write down what you have experienced when you have finished.

1 Begin by sitting upright in a comfortable chair, take a few slow deep breaths to calm and focus yourself, and close your eyes.

2 See yourself in a beautiful garden on a sunny afternoon. Feel the warmth of the sun on your skin and notice the flowers and butterflies. This is your own very special, magical garden, and you can come here whenever you want to do journey work.

3 There is a winding path running through the garden; you step on to it and start walking. As you walk, you see a small white temple in the distance. You walk up to the temple and before you is a dark, wooden door. As you look closer you see a marking on the door; remember this marking.

4 You push the door open and step over the threshold into a circular hall. In the centre of the hall is a circle of giant candles of every colour of the rainbow. You walk between the candles into the inner circle, when your attention is drawn to one of them.

5 Walk over to the candle that catches your attention and notice its colour. Ask the spirit of the candle if it has any message for you, or for any particular help that you need with your spellweaving. You may hear words, or see a picture or symbol in reply. You silently thank the spirit and the circle of candles gradually fades away.

6 Now you see the sunlight shining outside and you go back through the open door, down to the path, strolling back to your magical garden, filled with a sense of peace.

7 A soft mist begins to swirl around you, hiding the garden and the path, and gently guiding you back to your everyday world. Feel your feet on the floor and slowly open your eyes. Remember the marking on the door; this is your key to remind you of the message of the spirit of the candle.

The spells

This is where the magic really starts. This section contains more than thirty spells to bring a little sparkle into all areas of your life. The spells begin with meeting celestial angels and personal guides and

then you can start to work magic for healing and protection, self-empowerment, luck and prosperity, love and romance, friends and relationships, and much more.

Working with a variety of magical ingredients, including talismans, amulets, charms, spellbags and an assortment of

...to be good of heart is the true key to real magic...

stones, plants, herbs, trees and oils, you can begin to spellweave. Find out how to increase your aura of self-confidence, remove obstacles, improve your day-to-day business and

...the spells that follow are spells of beauty and power...

other affairs, enhance your career prospects, ensure safe travel, or attract the perfect mate. You can also clear negative vibes, find your direction in life and learn how to boost a flagging self-esteem.

Work with the phases of the moon to increase your psychic powers and strengthen your spellmaking abilities, and use the power of the sun for health, success and prosperity.

Seeking guidance

Witches were traditionally taught by a living teacher, the ancient knowledge being passed down from generation to generation. Today you can work with a teacher or find assistance in other ways. Use this spell to seek help.

you will need
- blue candle
- magical book
- paper
- black pen

best time
- waning moon
- Monday

preparation
The magical book can be any book that you feel contains important wisdom for you. This could be a book of sayings, or one that is associated with spiritual teachings, or even a book of poems or short stories. Select one that you feel particularly drawn to.

1 During a waning moon, light a blue candle and place it beside your magical book.

2 Concentrate on your need, writing it on a sheet of paper in black ink. Fold the paper into a narrow bookmark shape and say out loud:

I desire to find a path/teacher to lead me on the road to magic.

In this book I seek

In this book I peek.

Reveal a clue, now heed me.

3 Slide the paper into the book at random and open up the page you have found. Quickly read the words next to the paper, and don't be surprised if they contain important clues about your teacher or path.

4 Pinch out the candle and give thanks to the universal healing spirit for helping you in your quest.

Remember: when making magic, the clearer your intention, the more effective the result.

Below The universe will present you with the teacher who is best suited to you.

The guardian angel will guide you to do what is right for you when you listen and follow your "inner voice". To find your guardian angel, you need to work with the powers of creative visualization.

you will need

- white candle
- jasmine incense
- picture of angel or other heavenly being

best time

- any day of the week
- waxing moon

preparation

Find a comfortable chair and small table and sit where you won't be disturbed.

1 Light the white candle and jasmine incense and put the angel picture, or other heavenly being, on the table. Focus on the candle flame and say:

Angel fair, angel bright

Fill my life with your light.

2 Close your eyes and imagine a long ladder reaching up to the sky and see an angel coming down it towards you. Repeat the rhyme again and see the angel stand before you.

3 Repeat the rhyme for a third time and feel the angel's power flowing over you, and say:

Angel coming from above

I thank you deeply with my love.

The angel will fade away when it has finished blessing you.

4 Keep your eyes closed for a few more minutes, and then slowly bring yourself back into the room, feeling your feet on the floor. Get up and have a stretch, blowing out the candles and incense.

Right Guardian angels always want to help you, so never think that it is wrong to ask them for help for yourself, a relative or a friend.

guardian angel

The guardian angel is associated with the "fifth" element, ether or spirit. This angel presides over your sacred circle and is located at the centre rather than at one of the four quarters.

Angel blessings

In times of vulnerability, work with the power of the angels to bring blessings to yourself and others. Always remember to thank these Beings of Light – whether you sense their presence or not, they will be there.

you will need
- 2.7m (9ft) white cord
- white candle
- frankincense
- charcoal burner
- charcoal

best time
- anytime

1 Open your cord circle and place the candle, frankincense and charcoal burner in the centre. Turn to the south and light the candle and the charcoal burner. Add the frankincense to the hot charcoal saying:

*Lord of Light, this offering
I make.*

2 Next say the angelic invocation, touching your body as you do so:

Uriel above me,
[touch your head]

Michael beneath me,
[touch your stomach]

Raphael to my left,
[touch your left shoulder]

Gabriel to my right,
[touch your right shoulder]

By the power of these great angels

Surround me with light.

3 Visualize the four angels in the four directions: Uriel in the north, Michael in the south, Raphael in the east and Gabriel in the west. Bow your head and say "thank you" to acknowledge the presence of each one. Ask them for what you or someone you care about needs. This could be strength, courage, honesty, an open heart, or anything else to help you or the other person at this time.

4 When you have finished, say "thank you" again and let the angels depart. Blow out the candle and close your circle in the usual way.

Left Talk to the spirits as you would to a best friend and tell them what is on your mind. Do not simply gush out your problems and expect an answer.

Angel altar

It is not always necessary to cast a circle to make magic happen.

If someone you know is in need of angelic protection or healing, you can make an angel altar. Spellworkers use altars to make offerings.

you will need
- photograph of someone who needs healing
- white candle
- frankincense
- salt

best time
- anytime

1 Put the photograph, candle and frankincense within a circle of salt on top of your altar.

2 Light the candle and frankincense and say the Angelic Invocation (see opposite), touching the relevant parts of the body in the photo and saying the person's name. (If the photo doesn't show all the upper body, don't worry. Just touch the photo at the top, bottom, left, and right as you say the invocation.)

3 Visualize the four angels in the four directions. Greet them and say "thank you", and then ask each of them for a blessing for the person. When you have finished, say "thank you" again, and let the angels depart. Blow out the candle.

4 Leave the items on the altar for 24 hours, then remove the circle of salt, gathering it up so that it can be sprinkled on the earth outside. If it is a serious situation, wait another 24 hours and repeat steps 1-3 with new salt. You can keep repeating this every 48 hours until you feel your work is done.

altars

An altar is a sacred space and should not be used for any other purpose. It doesn't have to be big or complicated; a small table in the corner of the room will do, or an empty shelf. Keep the area clean and free of clutter.

Magic square of the sun

Each planet has its own magic square, which can be used to harness its powers. Magic squares use numerology to determine a special symbol called a "sigil". The magic square of the sun is used in this spell for health.

you will need
- 2.7m (9ft) white cord
- gold candle
- frankincense
- gold pen
- 15 cm (6 in) square of natural paper
- ruler

best time
- Sunday
- waxing or full moon

1 First, open your circle and place the gold candle and frankincense in the centre and light them. Sitting facing south inside the circle, translate the letters of your first name into numbers by using the numerology chart below. For example, the name Mary becomes 4197.

1	2	3	4	5	6	7	8	9
A	B	C	D	E	F	G	H	I
J	K	L	M	N	O	P	Q	R
S	T	U	V	W	X	Y	Z	

2 Use the Magic Square of the Sun chart to work out the sigil of your name by drawing a line through the appropriate numbers so that it forms a pattern.

3 Using the gold pen, mark a 7.5cm (3in) square in the top right-hand corner of the paper. Draw your sigil in this square. On the back of the paper, copy the sigil of the sun and write the words "Angel Och" (healing spirit of the sun).

4 Hold the piece of paper to your heart, with your sigil facing inwards, and visualize golden orange light, filling first your heart and then your whole body. Say:

I am healthy and well.

5 Then take a strand of your hair and lay it on the spell. Fold the piece of paper six times so that it forms a small packet with the hair inside. Keep it in a very safe place, or carry it with you, maybe wearing it next to your heart.

the magic square of the sun

6	32	3	34	35	1
7	11	27	28	8	30
19	14	16	15	23	24
18	20	22	21	17	13
25	29	10	9	26	12
36	5	33	4	2	31

Use the square to mark out the sigil of your name. The sigil for Mary (4197) has been added here as an example.

Above The sigil of the sun. Copy it on to your piece of paper to increase the power of the spell.

Psychic protection

If you are feeling permanently tired and low, it may be that you are picking up too much negativity from people and places around you, in which case you could possibly benefit from a little psychic protection.

you will need
- 12 tealights
- indigo blue candle
- myrrh incense or essential oil (and burner)
- carnelian stone
- vervain Bach flower essence or fresh sprig of vervain
- 15 cm (6 in) square of indigo cloth
- red thread

best time
- Saturday
- waxing moon

1 Arrange the tealights in a circle, and open the circle deosil, beginning in the east by lighting the first tealight.

2 Sit in a comfortable position in the centre of the circle facing west, and light the indigo candle and the incense or essential oil burner with a few drops of myrrh.

3 Close your eyes and allow your breathing to slow down and relax. As you do so, visualize yourself in a golden globe of pale blue light with orange flames around the circumference.

4 Take the carnelian stone and bring it to a point about 5cm (2in) below the navel. This is the hara, or power centre. Hold the stone on your hara and repeat the following invocation three times:

Bright angels of the astral plane, please come and bless this stone and fill it with your power, love and protection.

After the third time, say "thank you" to the angels and add "and so may it be".

5 Place the stone anointed with vervain Bach flower essence, or with a sprig of the fresh herb itself, on the indigo cloth and wrap it into a parcel. Tie it with red thread and carry the spell with you, or wear it next to your body.

6 Finish the spell by extinguishing the candle and myrrh, and then close the circle by blowing out the night lights, widdershins. Do not use the myrrh or the candle again, but dispose of them safely.

carnelian

This deep red or orange stone has the ability to protect you from negativity. It also helps to stabilize unbalanced energy in your surroundings. The stone is connected to the hara, or Shaman's Cave, and so links you to your own inner power and strength during times of psychic stress.

vervain

Considered sacred, vervain is also known as the "wizard's herb" and has been used for hundreds of years in casting spells and divination. It is used in magic to protect, enhance and purify. Anointing your magical equipment with vervain will ensure that both you and they are kept clean and protected.

Nature's healing powers

There's a close link between medicine and magic when you tap into the healing properties of nature's plants and trees. Invoke the powers of fresh green lime fruit to help restore health to yourself or another person.

you will need

- 2.7m (9ft) white cord
- gold candle
- gold pen
- 15cm (6in) square of natural paper
- knife
- lime
- gold thread
- 15cm (6in) square of orange fabric

best time

- Sunday

1 Open the circle and honour the four directions. Light the candle, saying:

Angel Och, healing spirit of the sun,
I light this flame to honour your
presence and ask you to hear this prayer.

2 Write your or another person's name with the gold pen on the paper, at the same time visualizing health and wellbeing surrounding you or them.

3 Cut the lime lengthways into two. Fold the paper three times and place between the two lime halves. Bind the pieces together with gold thread, saying:

Powers of lime

Health is mine/thine.

Cleanse the body, cleanse the mind,

Spirit pure, fill my [or person's name] *being*

With health, with health, with health.

4 Place the bound lime in the orange cloth and bind the cloth with gold thread. Close the circle in the usual way.

5 Bury the parcel in the earth under an ash, birch, juniper, orange or cedar tree. Ask the tree to help you (or another) to return to good health, and thank the tree.

Right The cedar tree's particular qualities and abilities include that of purification.

Stop the gossip

If you do anything that is a little out of the ordinary, there is a good chance that tongues will start to wag. If it becomes a problem, nip it in the bud with this spell and protect your reputation.

you will need
- 2.7m (9ft) white cord
- red candle
- red pen
- a very small square of natural paper
- snapdragon (antirrhinum) flower
- thorn
- red ribbon

best time
- Tuesday
- waning moon

preparation
Find a holly tree to bury your spell under. You might want to perform your spell next to it too, if the weather allows.

1 Open your cord circle. Light the red candle, face south and sit down.

2 Write in red pen on the paper square the name of the person, people, or organization that is gossiping about you. If you do not know the source of the gossip-mongering, write "whoever it is".

3 Carefully take one of the larger flower heads from the stem of the snapdragon and gently open it up. Fold the piece of paper or roll into a tiny scroll and place it inside the flower, repeating five times:

Speak only goodness, think only kind.
Look to your own faults, and not to mine.

4 Keep the scroll of paper in place by sealing the flower head with the thorn. As you do this say:

Flower seal, flower heal, lips that speak
not from the heart.

5 Take the spell to a holly tree, tell it of your intentions to bury it there and ask it to protect your good name.

6 Bury the snapdragon flower head under the holly tree and say "thank you" by tying a small red ribbon to a branch.

7 As you walk away, visualize that you are leaving the malicious gossip behind you. Do not look back.

snapdragons

In plant lore, snapdragons are associated with powerful people who misuse their power through verbal aggression and criticism. Snapdragons are used in magic to redirect "lower" energies, helping them to find a more creative and suitable outlet.

Below Holly is sacred to Mars. Use it to call for protection or to banish conflicts.

Mending a broken heart

It's more or less impossible to go through life without suffering. Whether you're dealing with the end of a love affair or not achieving a heartfelt desire, special healing is needed to help you through the grieving process.

you will need
- 16 tealight candles
- 1 pink candle
- rose essential oil
- oil burner
- pansy
- circular piece of natural paper
- glue
- 4 pieces of hair
- gold pen
- apple pips (seeds)

best time
- Sunday
- waning moon

1 Arrange the tealights in a circle and open the circle deosil, beginning in the west by lighting the first tealight. Sit in the centre of the circle facing south and light the pink candle and the oil burner to which have been added a couple of drops of rose essential oil.

2 Close your eyes and breathe in the soft fragrance of the rose essential oil. As you do so, imagine yourself surrounded by a pink light. This soft pink light permeates your whole being and fills the sacred circle where you are sitting.

3 Take the pansy and bring it to your heart. Hold it against your heart and in a soft voice tell it your troubles, tell it what is making you feel upset.

4 Now take your paper circle and stick the pansy at the centre with a little glue. Take the four pieces of hair and fix them so that they radiate out from the pansy in the four directions. Using the gold pen, write this healing prayer in a deosil direction, beginning in the west:

Pansy take away my pain

Heal my heart

So that I may gain [write down what it is you are asking for].

5 Keep repeating this rhyme, personalizing it in your own way, around the paper circle until you have about a 2cm (³/₄in) border. To finish your healing circle, stick the apple pips around the edge to make the border.

6 Close the magic circle in the usual way, giving thanks to the spirits for their healing. Keep your healing circle. You might like to cover it with tissue paper to protect it, or else display it near your altar.

Below Another name for the pansy is "heartsease", 'so-called' because of its reputed ability to ease a broken heart.

Removing obstacles

One of the most exciting ways of using magic is to clear away obstacles that stand in your way. Remember though that your spell must be for the "greatest good of all" and not done for purely selfish reasons.

you will need
• a gift for Mother Earth
• a fossil or blessed stone
• natural sea salt

best time
• Saturday
• fourth day after full moon

preparation
Carry your stone or fossil with you for seven days, from a Saturday to a Saturday, and tell it all your troubles. Perform the spell on the seventh day, Saturday. Choose a quiet spot outside where you feel comfortable and welcome to perform the spell.

1 Take your gift and fossil to your chosen spell spot. Starting in the east, use the salt to draw a deosil circle, large enough to sit in. Say the Light Invocation (see Angel Blessings).

2 Facing north, say this invocation to Mother Earth. Say it with as much feeling as possible and repeat three times:

Mother Earth, I bring you a gift of [say what your gift is] *because I have come today to ask you to help me. I wish to remove* [state your obstacle]. *I ask you with all my heart if you will talk with Cassiel, angel of Saturn, on my behalf and both of you help me to lift the condition by helping me to understand why it is here, so that I may move forward safe in the knowledge that I am part of a loving universe. Teach me, Mother Earth, to be wise and to trust in the beauty of all life. Show me the way to remove this obstacle so that I may grow in understanding and wisdom.* [Take your fossil.]

I ask that this fossil [or stone], *when it is buried in your being, may take away my burden and help me to endure, because it is within you and you are with me.*

3 Say "thank you" after the final round and bury your fossil or stone. Send the energies home by saying "and so may it be" while visualizing the completion of your task.

4 Starting in the west, break your circle of salt widdershins and brush it away into the surrounding area until you are back in the west again. Bury your gift and walk away, leaving your troubles buried behind you. Do not look back.

offerings

With spellweaving it is important to give, or you may not receive. Your gift for Mother Earth can be something you have made yourself, such as a cake or a picture you have painted. It doesn't matter what it is; what is important is how it was made: in a spirit of love and thanks.

Strengthening willpower

Making magic is about focusing your will to achieve a result. The more focused and determined you are, the better the likely outcome. Try this spell to strengthen your willpower.

you will need
- salt
- haematite stone
- wand
- red candle
- centaury flowers or Bach flower essence
- 12.5cm (5in) square of red cloth
- gold thread

best time
- Tuesday
- waxing moon

preparation
Place the haematite in a bowl of salt water overnight during a full moon. Store it in a dark place afterwards until you are ready to perform the spell.

1 Using your wand, cast a sacred circle beginning in the east. Put the red candle, centaury flowers or essence, cloth, thread and stone in the centre of the circle and light the candle.

2 Beginning in the east, hold the stone in your left hand and the candle in your right and pass the stone over the candle flame as you say:

I call the Sylphs, the helpers of air.
[then turn to the south]

I call the Salamanders, the helpers of fire.
[then turn to the west]

I call the Undines, the helpers of water.
[then turn to the north]

I call the Gnomes, the helpers of earth.

Sylphs, Salamanders, Undines and Gnomes, please bless this stone so that it may remind me that I have the mental power to achieve my goal [or say what particular goal you are trying to achieve], *sticking to what I feel is right for me. For I know that I am as firm and as steadfast as a rock.*

Right Centaury was traditionally renowned for its anti-demonic properties. Today the flower essence is used to strengthen willpower.

3 Now place the stone on the red cloth, together with the centaury flowers or a few drops of centaury essence. Bind the stone in the cloth with the golden thread.

4 Say "thank you" to your element helpers and let them depart. Blow out the candle and close the circle in the usual way.

5 Keep the amulet in your pocket and carry it with you. Whenever you feel weak-willed, holding on to it will remind you of your resolve.

Aura of confidence

Don't let a lack of self-confidence hold you back! If you spend too much time waiting in the wings and not enough on centre stage, give your confidence a boost with this spell.

you will need
- 2.7m (9ft) white cord
- gold candle
- gold pen
- 15cm (6in) square of natural paper
- larch Bach flower essence
- envelope
- gold ribbon
- tin box

best time
- Sunday
- waxing moon

preparation
Practise Golden Light Breathing before. Bury the spell by a hazel tree when you have finished.

1 Open the circle beginning in the east. Sit facing south, light the gold candle and say:

Oh Michael, Angel of the Sun, I call upon your presence and ask you to shine your golden light upon my life. Strengthen my aura with your positive rays.

2 Close your eyes and imagine that you are surrounded by an egg-shaped space. This is your aura. Breathing gently, watch as the Angel of the Sun beams his golden light rays towards you. With every in-breath feel the golden light warming and energizing your whole body. As you breathe out, see the egg-shaped space filling up and becoming bigger and brighter, as your aura expands outwards from your body. Feel yourself filled with the power of light and repeat the words "I can" to yourself six times.

3 Gently open your eyes and take the gold pen and write down six things that you would like to achieve in the next six months. Choose goals that seem just a little out of your reach at the moment, but not so far away as to make you feel they are impossible. Add six drops of larch essence to your goals, fold the paper, put it in the envelope and tie the gold ribbon around it.

Right The sun is the bringer of life, and you should visualize its rays filling your aura with optimism.

4 Blow out the candle, say "thank you" to Angel Michael and close the circle in the usual way.

5 Take your envelope and put it in the tin box. Bury the box under a hazel tree and leave it for six months. Do not look back.

6 After six months, you may go back to the tree, unearth the box and open the envelope. What progress have you made with your goals?

Banishing the demons

It is important to feel good about yourself. This is not about "putting on a show" for others, as true self-esteem springs from an inner sense of worth. If you suffer the demons of low self-esteem, try this banishing spell.

you will need
- 2.7m (9ft) white cord
- black candle
- black pen
- a sheet of natural paper
- juniper berry essential oil
- black thread
- heatproof container

best time
- Saturday
- waning moon

preparation
Find a suitable blackthorn or apple tree where you can bury the ashes when you have finished.

1 Cast a cord circle in the usual way, beginning in the east.

2 Sit facing north, light the black candle and say:

Oh Cassiel, Angel of Saturn, I light this flame in honour of your presence and ask you to lend me your help.

3 Take the black pen and a piece of paper, and start writing down all the negative things you think or believe about yourself. You could start by saying: "I don't like myself because" (and list the reasons), or find another way of writing down all the bad things you think about yourself. Take your time with this and let yourself feel whatever emotions are there.

4 Sprinkle three drops of juniper berry oil on the paper and make it into a roll, tying it up with the black thread.

5 Now take the paper roll and hold it to the candle flame. Have the heatproof container ready to hold the burning paper. As you light the paper, say:

Right Many cultures have evolved elaborate rituals and pantomimes for overcoming demons.

Cassiel burning,

Cassiel bright,

Please banish the demons

And my unhappy plight.

6 When the paper has finished burning, say "thank you" to Cassiel and blow out the candle. Close the circle in the usual way.

7 Take the burned paper ash to a blackthorn or an apple tree and bury it at its foot, silently asking the spirit of the tree for healing.

Clear vision

The path of life is never straightforward. With so many available options, it can be hard to know which direction to take. If you can't see the way forwards, call upon the spirit of the Eagle to help you gain some clarity.

you will need

- wand
- lock of your hair
- piece of chamois leather 20cm (8in) by 15cm (6in)
- hole puncher
- 30cm (12in) leather strip for threading
- selection of shells, beads and feathers
- wild oat Bach flower essence
- 3 hazelnuts

best time

- Spring Equinox best, but can be performed anytime in the year.
- Sunday
- waxing moon

1 Find a comfortable place to sit and work and assemble all your ingredients. Cast an invisible circle around you and sit facing east.

2 Close your eyes and invoke the spirit of the Eagle, saying:

Spirit of the Eagle come, Spirit of the Eagle come.

I call you Spirit of the Eagle,

Speedily, quickly, come.

Please accept this gift and lend me your power

So that I may see the way ahead.

Place the lock of your hair in front of you as a gift for the spirit of the Eagle and feel yourself filled with his power and vision.

3 Open your eyes and make a drawstring pouch with the chamois leather. Punch a row of holes big enough to thread the leather strip through along the 15cm (6in) sides, about 1cm (^{1}/2in) from the edge. Fold the material in half lengthways and join the two sides together by making two seams. Thread the leather strip through the holes at the top. Decorate the bag with a selection of shells, beads and feathers.

4 Sprinkle a few drops of the wild oat essence over the hazelnuts and put them in the pouch. Draw up the string.

5 Say "thank you" to the spirit of the Eagle and close the circle.

6 Take the lock of your hair and find a suitable spot in nature. Release the lock of hair into the wind, visualizing your spell being filled with the Eagle's blessings. Carry the pouch with you until you feel it has worked its magic.

Left and right The hazel was believed to be a tree of knowledge and hazelnuts were once revered as food of the gods.

Increasing abundance

There's no virtue in being poor. We live on a rich and fertile planet so it makes sense to share in nature's bounty. But in order for prosperity to come to you, you need first to give freely of yourself.

you will need
- 2.7m (9ft) white cord
- four pinches of tobacco
- gold candle
- blessed silver coin
- 15cm (6in) square of orange silk
- fresh spearmint leaves
- orange thread

best time
- Sunday
- waxing moon

preparation
Carry the coin with you for seven days from Sunday to Sunday. During the week, give something of yourself for free that costs time and energy, such as cleaning for a friend.

1 Open your circle in the east and make offerings of tobacco to each of the four directions. Stand in the centre of the circle and light the candle.

2 Take out your silver coin and hold it in the palm of your left hand. Hold the gold candle in the other hand and face south. Say the invocation, passing your coin through the flame of the candle six times:

O Angel Michael, I ask you to help me to understand the nature of abundance, that I may become wealthy in spirit, as well as in affluence. I ask you to bring me the riches that I need in order to live comfortably. I ask for the right amount of prosperity to fill my life that will meet my needs and so give the time and energy to use my gifts, to celebrate life and to help others in poverty or unhappiness. Grant me this and I will remember to give as I have received.

3 Say "thank you" after the request, and place the coin in the orange silk square with some spearmint leaves, and bind with orange thread. Carry this with you in your coin purse, or keep it in a tin box at home or somewhere else where it will be safe.

4 Moving widdershins from the north, gather up the tobacco, saying "thank you" to each of the four directions as you do so. When you have finished closing say "and so may it be" and visualize the spell being carried into the universe.

5 Give the tobacco back to the earth by placing it underneath a tree – preferably an almond, horse chestnut, oak or field maple.

Right Even witches like to live in abundance and have to make some effort towards prosperity!

Work with tree magic for a good luck spell. Perform this whenever you are leaving something behind and starting something new. This can be anything from taking exams or starting college, to a new job or moving house.

you will need
- small amethyst
- turquoise stone
- oak leaves
- cinquefoil essential oil
- sprig of rosemary
- spellbag

best time
- Thursday
- full moon

preparation
Find a suitable spellbag (a small drawstring pouch). Look in any New Age shop or stores selling hand-crafted goods, or even make your own. This spell is performed at an oak tree, so find a suitable one in your area.

1 Greet your oak tree and tell it your intentions. Place the small amethyst at its base as an offering. Walking deosil in a circle, repeat four times:

O Sachiel, Angel of Jupiter, I ask you to hear my call. Light my path, guide my actions, words and thoughts and those of all I am yet to meet, that by the power of your might, all will be fortunate to my sight.

Good fortune growing, growing, growing, growing.

2 Anoint the turquoise stone and leaves with cinquefoil oil, while visualizing yourself surrounded by the arms of the mighty oak tree.

3 Place the anointed turquoise stone, the sprig of rosemary and the oak leaves in your spellbag. Hold it up to the oak tree and say out loud:

Heart of Oak, you are my heart and with honour I shall carry you by my side.

Thank you.

Right The oak tree lives for hundreds of years and is a symbol of strength. It grants good fortune to all who seek its blessings and is also a guardian tree, offering protection and courage.

4 Carry your spell with you at all times when you are seeking good fortune, and store it carefully when not in use. You could also do this spell as a special gift for a friend, using their name in place of yours throughout.

amethyst

Generally a healing stone, amethyst is also very good for calming the mind and helping with meditation. As you use the stone you may become aware of an increased imagination and ability to visualize clearly.

Travel safely, travel well

Almost everyone likes to travel, whether short journeys to visit friends or overseas trips to experience different cultures. You can use this spell either for yourself or another embarking on a journey.

you will need
- 2.7m (9ft) white cord
- yellow candle
- aromatherapy burner
- lavender essential oil
- an unusual stone from your area
- yellow and violet paints
- artist's paintbrush

best time
- Wednesday

preparation
Find a stone that is different in some way from other stones in your area, perhaps in colour, shape or size. Take it home with you, remembering to ask permission of Mother Earth first.

1 Open your cord circle in the east and honour the four directions. Place the candle and oil burner in the centre of the circle and light them, adding a few drops of lavender oil to the burner.

2 Facing east, paint your stone bright yellow. When it is dry, draw a triangle in violet, with a line near its base, as shown right. This is the alchemical symbol for air.

3 Hold the stone up to the east and as you do so, say the invocation eight times, making sure that you say "thank you" after the eighth.

O Raphael, Angel of the East, fill this stone with your blessing and protection. I pray to you for a safe journey for me [or someone else's name]. *Guard me* [or other] *on the path this journey takes, until I* [or other] *can return.*

4 Close your spell and circle in the usual way. Carry your stone with you on your journey or, if for someone else, give it to them to carry. Return the stone to Mother Earth when the journey is ended.

Right Keep the witch's maxim and "travel safely, travel well".

air

The element air represents the wind for travellers. Use the alchemical symbol for air to make your own travel talisman.

Running smoothly

Most witches work for a living, and it is important that day-to-day affairs flow smoothly, bringing in sufficient income and job satisfaction, and leaving you enough time and energy to follow other interests.

you will need
- 3, 7 or 9 fresh basil leaves
- mint leaves
- bowl of spring water
- citrine stone
- dried ears of corn
- rice grains

best time
- monthly, on the first day of waxing moon

1 Bless the basil and mint leaves, the spring water, citrine, ears of corn and rice grains. Soak the basil leaves in the bowl of water for about one hour, stirring occasionally in a deosil direction.

2 Beginning to the right of the entrance at your place of work, walk deosil around the building or work area, sprinkling the aromatic water as you go and repeating the following invocation:

Business expand, business grow,

Secure and successful –

my dealings flow.

3 Bless the citrine, corn, rice and mint leaves again, then place the citrine where you keep your money or transactions. Offer the corn and the rice to the energies that are helping you with your day-to-day affairs, by sprinkling them in discreet places around your office or workplace.

4 Carry the mint leaves with you in your money pocket or purse. Replace them with fresh ones each time you re-work the spell.

Left Rice symbolizes new life and will encourage fertile opportunities in your business.

Bless this house

Traditionally it was customary to bless or consecrate the place where you live. If you have recently moved into a new home, perform this ritual cleansing and blessing ceremony to clear the space and make it yours.

you will need
- natural sea salt
- small bowl
- rose geranium essential oil
- white candle
- aromatherapy burner
- spring water
- a few grains of organic rice
- 15cm (6in) square of golden fabric

best time
- Sunday
- late morning and through midday
- waxing moon

preparation
This spell is best performed when you are at home alone.

1 Bless and consecrate yourself with Angel Blessings. Place the salt in the bowl. Starting in the top right-hand corner of your home, sprinkle a pinch of salt in the four corners of the room, and at all the corners of every door and window. Proceed deosil around your home, through every room. As you sprinkle the salt, repeat:

I cleanse and purify this room of all unnecessary or negative vibrations.

2 Take the rose geranium oil and light the white candle. Again, working deosil around your home, place the candle in the centre of each room. Anoint all the doors and windows with a little of the oil as you say the following:

I call upon the Angels of Light and Love to bless this home and all who enter here.

May love, happiness, and harmony prevail.

3 Place the candle in the centre of your main living room. Add six drops of rose geranium oil to the lit aromatherapy burner filled with spring water. Sit quietly, visualizing your home filled with the qualities that you desire.

Right Visualize the power of the essential oil clearing your home of all unwanted energies.

4 Let the candle burn down almost completely. Anoint it with rose geranium oil and sprinkle with rice as thanks to the helpful energies, then fold it into the gold fabric. Place the parcel beneath your front door mat or as close to your main entrance as possible, saying:

This I place so that all who enter here will be blessed.

5 Leave the parcel undisturbed until the next time you perform a cleansing or blessing ceremony.

Clearing negative vibes

Places harbour psychic energies, both positive and negative. If you have had lots of unwelcome visitors, or any sickness, quarrels or upsets in your home, it is a good idea to clear away any leftover negative vibes.

you will need
- pieces of flint
- 1 onion for each room
- red thread
- red fabric
- garlic clove
- rosemary sprigs
- red candle
- frankincense
- charcoal burner

best time
- Tuesday

1 Place the pieces of flint in the centre of your main living room, or the room where you feel the most comfortable and spend most of your waking hours. Ask the flints the following:

Please become my helpers in removing any negative psychic energy from my home.

I ask that you become the focus of any negativity towards this place and thank you for helping me.

2 Leave the flints alone to one side while you continue with the next stage. Peel one onion for each room in the house, and suspend each one on a red thread. Hang the onions at windows throughout your home, repeating the following:

I ask that this onion absorb all negative vibrations that are entering this place.

Thank you.

3 Leave the onions in place for seven days, then gather them up into the red fabric with a clove of garlic, making sure that you do not touch them with your bare skin. Tie the fabric with a red thread and take it outside the boundaries of your home, to a place in nature where you can bury it, saying:

Mother Earth, I bring you these for your cleansing touch.

4 Collect your pieces of flint and place one to either side of the doorways to your property. Place the others outside, in the corners of your property boundary, reaffirming your request that they absorb any negative psychic activity.

5 Place rosemary sprigs on all the windowsills, then light the red candle and frankincense. As they burn, visualize your home surrounded by a globe of golden light, with blue flames around the outside, and say:

Peace be in all universes – may all who wish harm be healed of their ignorance.

6 Do not use this candle again. Once the spell is completed, bury it as you did with the onions.

garlic

This pungent bulb is famous for its protective powers against a whole host of evil influences. The plant was dedicated to Hecate, the Greek goddess of witchcraft, famous for her knowledge of plant lore and her magical gardens in Colchis, on the shores of the Black Sea.

Finding what is lost

Wednesday is Mercury's day, and Mercury is the god of thieves.

If something is lost or has been stolen from you, use the powers of your imagination to recover what is lost.

you will need
- 20cm (8in) wand of hazel
- honeysuckle essential oil
- yellow cloth

best time
- Wednesday
- waxing moon

preparation
Find a hazel tree and ask its permission for you to cut a wand. Take it gently and say "thank you". Leave the tree a lock of your hair in return as a gift. Bless the wand before you use it.

1 Find a quiet place where you won't be disturbed and draw a deosil circle around yourself with the hazel wand, saying:

By the powers of heaven and earth, I cast this sacred circle in the name of love, light, wisdom and truth.

2 Perform the Golden Light Breathing exercise and then anoint your temples, forehead and hands with honeysuckle oil. Sit or stand in the north, facing south and imagine that you are sitting upon a high mountain made of magnetic crystals. You can see for miles in any direction.

3 Visualize yourself opening your hands, so that the palms are facing upwards. Let us say that you have lost your keys. Say the following invocation:

Swift and sure, my keys return to me.

4 Imagine that your keys are being drawn back to you, by the strength of the magnetic mountain. Draw them back with as much willpower and concentrated thought as you can. Note any pictures that come into your mind and from which direction your keys return to your hands in the visualization.

5 To add to the spell's effectiveness, write what you have lost on a piece of paper and pin it up somewhere where you will see it until the object returns. If the lost object is in someone else's possession, he/she should feel compelled to return it quickly. If nothing happens, you can try the spell again in a week's time, or accept that the item is lost at this time.

6 Say "thank you" as usual to the energies that have helped you. Close your spell then move your hand widdershins from the end to the beginning of the original circle, saying:

This spell is done.

7 Wrap the hazel wand in the yellow cloth and add it to your magic kit. Keep this in a safe place.

hazel

The hazel tree has a long association with magic and divination. Forked hazel twigs have been used for hundreds of years to divine water. A wand made of hazel is very popular as it increases the magic of spells as well as giving protection during a ceremony.

Whenever you have anything to sell – whether it's something big like a house or a car or small items such as clothing or specialist equipment – you can use the power of magic to help "make it go".

you will need

- yellow flowers
- lavender incense or essential oil
- something to represent the item you are selling (e.g. a key for a car or house, or a picture of the item)
- yellow ribbon

best time

- Wednesday
- waxing moon

preparation

Take the item that you are selling and clean it thoroughly, saying:

Now is the time for us to part, with thanks I cleanse you.

1 Hold your item (or representation of it) in your right hand. Stand in front of your altar and turn to face west, the direction for letting go. As you say the invocation, turn from west to east, moving deosil:

I let go of this [say what it is], *so that something new can come in its place.*

2 Place a vase of yellow flowers on the altar and burn some lavender incense or essential oil. Tell the spirit of the item you are selling that you wish to part company, and need the new keepers to come and take over from you.

3 Tie up the item (or symbolic representation) with yellow ribbon and put it on your altar in the east. Call upon the East Wind to help you:

Hail to thee East Wind. This [name the object] *sells, this* [name the object] *sells.*

Here is the [name the item that represents the object] *to guide the next keeper here.*

May they come speedily and give me a satisfactory amount of money for this item, so that it may go to a new owner and I am free for something new.

4 Say "thank you" to the East Wind, adding:

This is for the highest good of all concerned.

flowers of the week

To enhance the magic of this spell, change the vase of flowers on the altar each day of the week for one week. Repeat the spell if the item hasn't sold, and repeat weekly until it goes.

Saturday	evergreens, cypress
Sunday	orange flowers
Monday	white flowers, river plants
Tuesday	red flowers
Wednesday	yellow flowers
Thursday	violet or purple flowers
Friday	pink flowers, roses

Below Orange is the colour for Sunday and solar magic, which will help you attract success.

Dream lover

Fed up with being single? Try spellweaving for your perfect love match.

Remember – do not name anyone, as you cannot control someone else's

free will. Trust that whoever answers will be right for your needs.

you will need

- bottle of rose water
- 2.7m (9ft) white cord
- 4 green candles
- charcoal and
  heatproof burner
- pink candle
- rose petals
- rose essential oil
- cinnamon stick
- gold pen
- glass bowl of spring
  water

best time

- Friday
- waxing moon

preparation

Take a long bath or shower first, then spray your whole body with rose water.

1 Open your cord circle. Light a green candle in each direction and invoking all the winds in turn:

Hail to thee East/South/West/North Wind. I call for love and make this offering of light to you.

2 Place some charcoal in the heatproof burner in the centre of the circle and light it. Light a pink candle next to it. Begin doing Golden Light Breathing until you feel charged and full of energy.

3 Facing east, put seven rose petals to one side, then rub a little rose oil into the rest. Crush the cinnamon stick and place with the scented rose petals on the burning charcoal.

4 Focus your heart upon feeling love. Write the word "love" in gold ink upon the seven petals you put to one side. Place them gently on the bowl of water.

5 Sit in the circle, breathing in the scent of rose and cinnamon. Take time to centre yourself and build up charged energy. Open your hands, open your heart, and speak your request seven times, with as much feeling as possible:

O Anael, Angel of Venus, I call upon you to fill me with love that I may feel a joyous heart. I ask that I may share this love with another who will come to me of his/her free will and together we shall know the beauty of a loving union. I ask this for the highest good of all.

6 Say "thank you" at the end of the seventh request. Blow out the candles, close your spell and then your cord circle, widdershins. Pour the rose petals and water respectfully upon the earth, or in a container of earth.

Below Queen Cleopatra understood the power of the rose to attract a mate. She is alleged to have strewn red rose petals several feet deep around her bed when she first met Mark Antony.

Magnetic attraction

If it's other people that have all the luck in attracting a mate and you're feeling left out, it's time to find your powers of magnetic attraction. This spell will spice up your life and draw your partner to you in a magical way.

you will need
- wand
- gold candle
- spellbag
- 6 sunflower seeds
- 15cm (6in) square of natural paper
- gold pen
- magnet
- passport-sized photograph of yourself

best time
- Sunday
- full moon

preparation
Find or make a suitable spellbag. This spell works with sun magic, so an orange or gold bag decorated with spirals would work well.

1 Cast a magic circle with your wand. Put the sunflower seeds and the gold candle in the south. Light the candle. Hold the seeds in the light of the candle and say:

Spirit of the sun, spirit of the sun, please come today and light the way. Lend me your power of light, that it may attract the wise and the bright into my life, easily, happily and for the good of all.

2 Put the sunflower seeds into the spellbag. Close your eyes and think about the type of person you are most looking to attract. When you are ready, open your eyes and write:

I [write your name] *am now ready and willing to attract the following person into my life.*

Go on to describe the kind of person you are looking for but don't name anyone in particular. Add "and so may it be" and sign the paper. Fold or roll it into a scroll and put it in the spellbag.

3 Take the magnet in your left hand and the photograph of yourself in the right. Pass your hands over the candle flame six times, saying:

Bless this magnet of love and friendship, that I may become a source of warmth and light. Let me now attract [say what kind of partner you are looking for].

4 Put the magnet and the photograph into the spellbag. Close up the spellbag and blow out the candle, thanking the spirit of the sun for helping you, and adding "this is for the highest good of all concerned". Close the circle.

5 Either keep the spellbag with you, or else put it on your altar next to a bunch of sunflowers or other gold or yellow flowers, and wait for the magic to happen.

Below Give plenty of consideration to your description of your ideal partner and be careful what you ask for, you might just get it!

Joining in love

Making charms is another way of making spells. For a romance that is blossoming, work with the energies of Spring and create this love token. Give it to your partner to make sure that your lives are intertwined.

you will need
- wand
- straight wooden stick
- knife
- two green ribbons
- two yellow ribbons
- thread or wool (yarn)
- beads, pendants or stones for decoration

best time
- Sunday
- Beltane sabbat, but may make the love charm at other times in the year at full moon.

preparation
For the love charm, find and smooth a fairly straight stick, of about pencil length.

1 Find a comfortable place to sit and work and cast an invisible sacred circle using your wand. Assemble all your materials in the centre of the circle and sit facing south.

2 Invoke the winds of the four directions, saying:

Hail to thee South/West/North/East Wind. I call upon your assistance in the making of this charm for [say the names]. *Please lend it your power, and give it your blessings and protection, for the highest good of all concerned.*

3 Now take the lengths of ribbon and secure them around the top of the stick using the thread or wool (yarn). Hold the stick firmly in place and lay out the ribbons in the four directions, green in the north and south, yellow in the west and east. You will want to wind the north and south ribbons deosil, and the east and west ribbons widdershins around the wood.

4 Weave the north ribbon over the east one, and the south ribbon over the west one. Repeat weaving the ribbons around the stick, crossing alternate adjacent pairs in a continuous pattern until you reach the base.

5 Secure the ends with thread or more ribbon. You can either leave the ribbon ends free, or tie beads, pendants or stones on to them as decoration.

6 When you have finished, say "thank you" to the Four Winds for helping you. Close the circle in the usual way.

Above This love charm is inspired by the Maypole, an ancient fertility symbol. During the Spring May Day festival (Beltane), people traditionally danced around the pole, interweaving coloured ribbons as they did so, symbolizing the joining of the male and female together.

New friends

Our friendships are the food of life and a good friend is worth their weight in gold. But there are times, such as when we change jobs or move area for instance, when we need to put in a bit of extra effort to make new friends.

you will need
- 2.7m (9ft) white cord
- 7 green candles
- aromatherapy burner
- sweet pea essential oil, diluted in sesame oil
- 5 pips (seeds) from a sweet organic apple
- gold pen
- natural paper

best time
- Friday
- waxing moon

preparation
Bathe and then massage your body with diluted sweet pea oil.

1 Open the cord circle in the east. Place the green candles in a horseshoe shape, with the open end facing north and you facing south in front of it.

2 Place the aromatherapy burner in the centre of the horseshoe shape and add 7 drops of sweet pea oil. Lay the apple seeds in the centre too. Light the first candle to your left and say:

Nogah, Nogah, Venus, Venus, light of love,
I honour and illuminate your beauty and
call upon you to help me today.

3 Light the next candle with the lit one, then put the first candle down. Continue this way until every single one is lit. Now light the aromatherapy burner.

4 Take the gold pen and write down your wish on the paper as follows:

By the powers of the four directions, above
me and below me, within me and without,
I call for favour with Anael, Angel of Venus,
I call for friends of the same heart that joy
and celebration shall prevail.

5 Pick up your wish and burn it in the flames of the last candle that you lit, visualizing as you do so that your wish is being carried to the skies.

6 Blow out the candles widdershins, saying on the last one "and so may it be". Close your circle in the usual way. Take the apple seeds to a prepared site or pot and dedicate them:

Nogah, these apple seeds I plant to honour
you and please you. And as they grow, so is
my life blessed with joy of friendships new.

sweet pea

In plant lore, the softly fragranced sweet pea is associated with bringing people together. This flower is for the loner or the outsider who finds it hard to feel connected with others. Use its magic to foster friendships.

When two people get together it is not always easy to come to an agreement, particularly on difficult issues. Nip any festering resentments in the bud with this spell to remove conflicts.

you will need
- 5.5m (18ft) white cord
- a small round table
- 5 red candles
- charcoal
- heatproof container
- coriander seeds
- red pen
- two pieces of natural paper

best time
- Tuesday
- waning moon

preparation
This spell works best if both partners do it together. But if the other is unwilling, you can still do it by yourself, writing down what it is you wish to let go of.

1 Open your cord circle. Place the round table or a round stool in the centre and on it position the red candles, also in a circle, and light them, remembering which candle is the last to be lit.

2 Light the charcoal in the heatproof container. When it is hot, face west and sprinkle on the coriander seeds, saying:

O Zamael, Angel of Mars, we call upon you to help us today/tonight, and dedicate this offering to you.

3 Breathe in the aroma of the burning seeds. Each person should then use the red pen to write on their piece of paper the emotion they want to let go of – jealousy, anger, hurt, etc.

4 Swap papers and add your negative feelings on the other side of the other's paper (without looking at what they have written). Then walk widdershins around the table five times, visualizing your emotion and the way you express it.

5 After you have circled the table for the fifth time, each of you should burn your own piece of paper in the flame of the last candle that was lit.

Making a wish together

Write your names down together on natural paper, stating a positive wish you both want. Place it in the centre of an organic apple cut in half. Seal with green candle wax and bury it near to the house in a prepared spot. If the apple pips (seeds) grow, tend them carefully because they represent new growth in your relationship that needs nurture.

Left The smoke from burning coriander seeds will help clear the air between two people in times of communication breakdown.

Cutting the ties

Facing up to the end of a love affair or friendship and saying goodbye or bidding farewell to a departed loved one is often painful. This spell helps to ease the pain of separation or mourning.

you will need
- purple altar cloth
- oil burner
- cypress essential oil
- white candle
- black candle
- 2 photos, one of yourself, one of the other
- 30 cm (12 in) black ribbon
- scissors

best time
- Saturday
- day before new moon

preparation
Clean and prepare your altar space and put the purple cloth on top. Clean the scissors in salt water and with a soft cloth polish the surface.

1 Place the oil burner in the middle of the altar towards the back. Light the burner and add three drops of cypress oil.

2 Tie one end of the black ribbon around the white candle, and the other around the black candle. Position the candles on the altar so that the ribbon forms a "tightrope" and place the two photographs side by side in the middle of the altar, underneath the ribbon, the one representing you on the side of the white candle, the one representing the other party on the side of the black.

3 Light the white candle and say:

White Candle, please hear my plea and represent me.

Help me to part from [say the other's name] *in a spirit of love and friendship.*

4 Light the black candle and say:

Black Candle, please hear my plea and represent [say the other's name].

Help [say the other's name] *to part from me in a spirit of love and friendship.*

5 Take the scissors and hold them over the taut ribbon. Prepare to cut the ribbon by saying:

Scissors shiny, scissors sharp,

Make me and [say the other's name] *move apart.* [cut the ribbon]

Neither harmed nor alarmed

May we now go our separate ways.

Scissors clean, scissors new,

Make a clean break.

6 Put the white candle on top of your photograph, the black one on top of the other person's picture. Burn the candles for three minutes, visualizing you and the other person happily walking away from each other.

7 Open your eyes and move the photographs a little further apart and repeat the visualization. Repeat once more. Close the spell by saying "thank you" to the spirits and blow out the oil burner. Repeat the spell for up to seven days.

cypress

The Egyptians and Romans of ancient times dedicated the cypress tree to the gods of death and the afterlife. The tree is often found in cemeteries, planted to help departed souls find their way into the next world.

Drawing down the moon

The moon is the protector and guardian of women. Draw on her powers to refresh and rejuvenate you for the month ahead, or if you are a man, to help you get more in touch with your sensitivity and powers of intuition.

you will need
- 13 circular stones, river stones or crystals
- salt
- aromatherapy burner
- jasmine essential oil
- 9 white or cream candles

best time
- up to two days before full moon

1 Beginning in the south, lay down 12 of your chosen stones in a deosil direction (it doesn't matter whether or not the stones are the same size as one another). Place the 13th stone in the centre.

2 Sprinkle the stones with a little salt. Light the burner and put in three drops of jasmine oil.

3 Place eight candles around the circle, and one by the centre stone. As you light the candles say:

*Magna Dea, Light of the Night, I light
these candles to guide your moonrays here.
I ask you to come and bless this circle.*

4 Facing south, stand with your arms outstretched above your head and your feet quite wide apart. Reach towards the sky. Say the lunar invocation:

*Hail to thee, Sophia, holy spirit of the
wise moon. I call upon you to enter and
fill me with your light. Protect me and
guide me on the moonway. Teach me your
wisdom and truth as I seek your clarity
and guidance.*

5 Imagine drawing down the powers of the moon into yourself. Allow yourself to be refreshed and refilled with the feminine virtues of wisdom, beauty and grace. Let the moon bless your feelings and perceptions until you feel energized and content. Bring your arms down to your sides.

6 Close your circle widdershins, saying "thank you" as you blow out the candles. Dispose of any organic ingredients in a safe place outside.

Below Both men and women are intimately linked to the changing faces of the moon as it progresses through its cycle.

Lunar wishes

A talisman is a written wish and can take any form. Make a lunar talisman to draw on the powers of the moon. Remember: a new to full moon is the time for drawing things to you; a full to dark moon is the time for letting go.

you will need
- wand
- 2 silver or white candles
- moonstone
- silver pen
- ruler
- 23cm (9in) square of natural paper

best time
- Monday
- time your spell according to the correct moon phase for attracting or releasing something.

1 Open a sacred circle and put your spell ingredients in the centre. Facing north, light the candles, saying as you do so:

Hail to you Levanah, I light these candles in your honour and ask for your assistance this night.

2 Translate your first name into numbers using the chart below. For example the name Isabel becomes 911253. Then work out the sigil for your name by tracing the shape of those numbers on the Kamea of the Moon. Draw a 5cm (2in) square in the top left-hand corner of the paper with the silver pen and copy your sigil into it. Write your wish in the remaining space.

1	2	3	4	5	6	7	8	9
A	B	C	D	E	F	G	H	I
J	K	L	M	N	O	P	Q	R
S	T	U	V	W	X	Y	Z	

3 Fold the four corners of the paper into the centre, then repeat twice more.

4 Hold the moonstone next to your stomach and silently ask:

Levanah, I offer this moonstone in your honour, and ask that you imbue it with your power to make my wish come true.

5 When you have finished, say "thank you" and close the circle in the usual way. If your talisman is for an "attracting something to you" wish, leave it, together with the moonstone, in the light of the increasing moon until your wish is granted. If it is for a "letting go of something" wish, take the talisman and stone to a river or seashore on the first night after full moon and place it in the water to be taken away. Watch it leave, and then turn away. Do not look back.

kamea of the moon

In magic, the moon is associated with the number nine. Use its powers to create a special moon talisman for enhancing perception and increasing psychic powers. The sigil for Isabel has been added as an example. The sigil should always begin as a circle and end in a line.

37	78	29	70	21	62	13	54	5
6	38	79	30	71	22	63	14	46
47	7	39	80	31	72	23	55	15
16	48	8	40	81	32	64	24	56
57	17	48	9	41	73	33	65	25
26	58	18	50	1	42	74	34	66
67	27	59	10	51	2	43	75	35
36	68	19	60	11	52	3	44	76
77	28	69	20	61	12	53	4	45

Let it shine

If you feel you are hiding your light or that others simply don't notice you, it's easy to become discouraged. Work with the powers of the moon to bring yourself out of the darkness and receive the recognition you deserve.

you will need
- silver altar cloth
- 3 silver or white candles
- natural paper
- silver pen
- envelope
- silver or glass bowl of spring water

best time
- full moon

preparation
This spell uses an altar. In the evening when the moon has risen, prepare your altar by blessing and laying out your equipment. Arrange the candles in a crescent shape to symbolize the moon.

1 Light the three candles from left to right saying:

Moon Maiden inspire me, Moon Mother protect me, Moon Matriarch empower me, as I ask this favour. At this hour of bright moonlight, please help me to shine at what I do, and to receive fitting reward for my efforts.

2 Close your eyes and really focus on what it is you need and are trying to achieve; this could be a promotion at work, or a pay rise, or simply for your friends to take more notice of you. Take the silver pen and write out your exact and precise need.

3 Fold the paper and put it in the envelope and seal it carefully. Hold the envelope below each candle in turn, so that the light of the candle shines on it. Be careful not to let the paper singe or burn.

4 Sprinkle the envelope with water in front of each of the three candles from left to right in turn, saying:

Moon Maiden bless me, Moon Mother guide me and Moon Matriarch assist me that my will be done.

5 Blow out the candles from left to right, giving thanks to each aspect of the moon in turn.

6 Hide the envelope away until the next full moon. You may be surprised at the results. If it is a particularly persistent problem, you may need to keep working with this spell every month at full moon.

Below As this is a moon ritual, you need to set out your altar accordingly with white and silver items to represent her.

Opening the inner gates

The gate of inner vision, or the "third eye", is situated on the forehead just above the eyebrows. When this gate is open, it gives you access to inner vision and enhanced psychic power.

you will need
- 2.7m (9ft) white cord
- flower
- red candle
- small bowl of water
- stone
- sandalwood incense
- a picture of an open door or gate

best time
- Monday
- waxing moon

1 Open your cord circle and place the flower in the east, the candle in the south, the bowl of water in the west and the stone in the north. Light the incense in the centre of the circle.

2 Sit in the centre with the picture of the open door or gate on your lap. Close your eyes, centre yourself and focus on your intention: be sure that your wish to work with inner vision is for the highest good of all.

3 Stand up and make opening gestures to each of the four quarters. Say the following as you pick up each object:

Open my mind like a growing flower, may my vision now empower,

Open my mind to the candle fire, may my vision now inspire, [light the candle]

Open my mind to the water's flow, that on vision journeys I may go

Open my mind to this stone so cold, that visions I shall safely hold.

Right Use the power of the light of the moon to enhance your psychic ability and inner vision.

4 Pick up the open gate or door picture and hold it out in front of your heart. Circle or turn around four times saying:

Open gates that I may roam

Safely bring my knowledge home.

5 Sit down and close your eyes again. Relax and sit in meditation for a while, letting any pictures or images come and go. When you are ready, open your eyes and put out the incense, and close the circle widdershins.

6 Keep a record of what you have experienced in words and/or pictures.

Index

air 16, 17, 48
altars 35
amulets 30, 36, 37, 42, 46
angels 11, 30, 34, 35
   guardian angels 17, 33
animals 10, 11

Beltane 12, 13, 16
birds 10, 11
blessings 23, 34, 50

candles 20, 22
career 16, 31, 49
charms 30, 38, 39, 41, 56
circles 24–5
clothes 22
colour 10, 14
crystals 10, 11, 21

days of the week 19, 52
dreaming 15, 28

earth 10, 11, 16, 17
elements 9, 16–17, 33
energy 10, 11

equinoxes 12, 13
esbats 15
essential oils 21, 22, 31

feathers 11, 25
fertility 11, 16
festivals 8–9, 12–13, 15
finding what is lost 52
fire 16, 17
friendships 7, 16, 30, 57

gems 10, 11
golden light breathing 22, 52
gossip 39
guidance 30, 32

healing 7, 14, 30, 31, 35,
   36, 38
   emotional 11, 16, 40
herbs 21, 31, 37

Imbolc (Candlemas) 12,
   13, 16
incense 20–1
inner journeys 9, 29
intuition 15, 16

Lammas 12, 13, 16

life direction 11, 31, 45
light 10, 14
love 11, 30, 31, 54, 55, 56
luck 30

meditation 9, 26–7
moon 9, 10, 14, 60, 61, 62

nature 8, 10, 38
negativity 11, 31, 51

obstacles 31, 41, 49
offerings 25, 35, 41
opportunities 7, 31

pentacles 17
planets 8, 10, 11, 18, 19
plants 10, 31, 38, 39, 40, 51,
   52, 53, 57, 59
preparation rituals 9, 22
prosperity 11, 16, 30, 31, 46
protection 11, 30, 35, 37
psychic powers 11, 15, 16,
   31, 63

relationships 30, 58, 59
rocks 10, 21
romance 16, 30, 31, 54,
   55, 56

sabbats 12–13, 14, 16
sacred space 24–5, 35
salt 20, 24, 25
Samhain (Hallowe'en) 12,
   13, 16
scrying 9, 28
seasons 8, 12–13
self-confidence 30, 31, 43,
   44, 62
selling property 53
smudging 22
solstices 12, 13
spellbags 21, 30, 45, 47, 55
spells 7, 9, 11, 18, 19
   spellweaver's pledge 23
stars 8, 10, 11, 18

stones 10, 11, 21, 31, 37,
   47, 48
success 31
sun 9, 14, 31, 36

talismans 30, 48, 61
three, law of 7, 23
tools 9, 20–1
travel 16, 31, 48
trees 10, 11, 31, 38, 47

vibrations 10, 11, 31, 51

wands 20, 52
water 16, 17
Wheel of the Year 12–13, 14
white cord 20, 24, 25
willpower 42
witches 7, 8, 10
   rules of conduct 25
writing materials 20, 32,
   36, 42

zodiac 18–19

Acknowledgements

Photography by Peter
Anderson, Simon Bottomley,
Jonathan Buckley, John
Freeman, Michelle Garrett,
Don Last, William Lingwood,
Gloria Nicol, Debbie Patterson,
Fiona Pragoff, Peter Williams
and Polly Wreford.